CW00539385

MY KIND OF CLUB

MY KIND OF CLUB

The Inside Story Of Neil Warnock's Cardiff City

By Dominic Booth

Reach Sport

www.reachsport.com

Reach **Sport**

www.reachsport.com

Copyright © Dominic Booth 2020.

The right of Dominic Booth to be identified as the owner of this work has been asserted in accordance with the Copyright, Designs and Patents Act, 1988.

All Rights Reserved. No part of this publication may be reproduced, stored in a retrieval system, or transmitted in any form, or by any means,electronic, mechanical, photocopying, recording or otherwise without the prior permission in writing of the copyright holders, nor be otherwise circulated in any form of binding or cover other than in which it is published and without a similar condition being imposed on the subsequent publisher.

Published in Great Britain and Ireland in 2020 by
Reach Sport, a Reach PLC business,
5 St Paul's Square, Liverpool, L3 9SJ.

www.reachsport.com
@Reach_Sport

Reach Sport is a part of Reach PLC.
One Canada Square, Canary Wharf, London, E15 5AP.

Hardback ISBN: 978-1-911613-86-2
eBook ISBN: 978-1-911613-90-9

Photographic acknowledgements:
Reach PLC, PA Images.

Design and typesetting by Reach Sport.
Book editing: Simon Monk.

Printed and bound by CPI Group (UK) Ltd,
Croydon, CR0 4YY.

Contents

Acknowledgements

First of all, I must say a massive thank you to Neil Warnock. Without him, this book obviously wouldn't exist. It was a genuine pleasure to cover Cardiff City while Neil was in charge. And as he says in the foreword he was kind enough to write, it's never dull when he is manager of a club, but as a young journalist I really appreciated the time he gave me every week – even the times he called to tell me I was way off the mark!

Thankfully, Neil and I maintain an excellent relationship, so he was happy to lend some more of his time to go over everything about his Cardiff tenure; the good, the bad and of course the tragic.

Thanks must also go to Steve Hanrahan, Simon Monk, Paul Dove, Claire Brown, Harri Aston and all

ACKNOWLEDGEMENTS

at Reach Sport for their help in bringing the book to publication. Also a special mention to Rick Cooke, who produced a cover that says everything about Warnock and his Cardiff City tenure.

I'd also like to thank those people who wanted to publish the book but didn't, for different reasons. Your interest and encouragement persuaded me that this wasn't such a crazy idea. You know who you are!

I asked a few people for advice before delving into the writing process. Peter Miller was a fountain of knowledge about the book industry, Aled Blake provided some useful advice as well as a fan's perspective, while Paul Abbandonato, Matthew Southcombe and Jamie Kemble all helped too. Simon Edwards is a great friend and a brilliant gauge of how Bluebirds fans feel about any given topic.

I was lucky enough to speak to Sol Bamba and happily he was his usual charismatic and talkative self, which was a great help. Greg Halford's input was greatly appreciated too. I'd also like to thank the Cardiff players and staff I interviewed while at *WalesOnline*, some of whom feature here, the likes of Joe Bennett, Kevin Blackwell and Sean Morrison.

Nathan Blake is a legend not only in the eyes of Cardiff

fans, but in my personal view too, as a former podcast colleague and someone who always tells it straight. Glen Williams and Ian Mitchelmore are both top guys too and do fantastic work at *WalesOnline*. Thanks all.

Finally, my deepest thanks go to my father Jonathan Booth and my fiancee Amelia Lumb, who both helped more than they will admit or maybe realise. All my family, in fact, encouraged me to pursue this book and I'm so glad they did.

Thanks all and I hope you enjoy reading the book.

Dominic Booth

Dominic Booth is an experienced football journalist and former Cardiff City correspondent for WalesOnline. He followed the Bluebirds the length and breadth of the country during Neil Warnock's time in charge and built a strong rapport with the manager. He now covers Manchester United at the Manchester Evening News.

Foreword by Neil Warnock

When a football manager arrives at a club, he is faced with a brand new set of journalists who cover them, and he's not aware of any of the attributes they have.

In the olden days when I took over a club, I used to speak to the local journalist and even took them on the bus to away games to let them see for themselves what the team was all about. I would tell them everything, literally everything.

But of course the bits I would say 'off the record', they would keep in confidence. As the years have gone by, unfortunately, with editors especially in the national tabloids demanding headlines, those words 'off the record' seem to be a thing of the past.

Arriving at Cardiff City however, I met Dominic Booth, then of *WalesOnline* and the *South Wales Echo*, and was struck by his enthusiasm and knowledge. And over the years I enjoyed a rapport with him and indeed have used the phrase 'off the record' numerous times – and he has never let me down. His reporting of games appeared the same as I felt for the most of the time.

I only had to phone him very occasionally when I thought he was a little harsh with his ratings of certain players and their performances! This book is a very good recollection of my time at the club, both the ups and the downs, in Dominic's own words. He obviously used my press conferences to set the tone and, I have to say, at the time I wondered why he was so attentive in those meetings. Well, now I know!

I think it's great when a young man decides to write a book and there's usually never a dull moment when I'm in charge of a club. I dealt with Dominic on a daily basis and I've always appreciated the job that local journalists have and why, when I see a missed call on my phone, I always try and call back as I realise they have a job to do. It's not something most managers do, I can assure you.

It's nice for me to go back in time to arriving at the club in October 2016 and to relive some of the unforgettable times that we have had. I think it's fair to say Cardiff City was a fragmented club at that time and I will always be proud of putting all the parts back together again.

We had some tremendous highs and, as always, some extremely difficult periods. But the club has thrived and will continue to do so in the future because of the diehard fans who support their beloved Bluebirds through thick and thin. Writing this in 2020, with all the difficulties this year has contained, I have to admit I've never witnessed a more testing time for football in general and we will not know the consequences for many a year.

But one thing I do know is that Cardiff City will still be a great club, both on and off the field, and that is why I hope you all enjoy Dominic's own words to describe what has been one of the most fulfilling jobs I've ever done in football, while at the same time including the saddest period for me also.

So thank you once again to Dominic for putting it all down on paper and I hope you enjoy reading it.

Be lucky.

Neil Warnock

Prologue

"Natalie, sorry love. I'm in a press conference. I love you too... thank you darling. Enjoy Australia, bye darling."

It was the most fitting Neil Warnock moment you could wish for and it came on a day both he and Cardiff City fans had been dreaming about for 18 months.

Warnock would, of course, call his eldest daughter back. She was telephoning from the middle of the night on the other side of the world to congratulate her father on his latest miracle. This was the day Cardiff City achieved promotion to the Premier League and, unlike his daughter, the manager's timing was perfect.

The minutiae of the actual match, few will remember. A rather tedious 0-0 draw with Reading was to be enough, as Fulham folded at Birmingham City to allow the

Bluebirds to claim second place in the Championship and automatic promotion behind league winners Wolves.

When supporters look back, most memorable will be the feeling, the glory of the sensational celebrations that would follow in picture-perfect conditions. It was a baking hot day in Cardiff in which supporters basked not only in the glorious heat, but their team's tremendous triumph.

You only had to romp around the city later that day to catch clutches of delirious blue-clad supporters in total euphoria.

Their team had achieved the impossible and it was thanks to one man, the champagne-soaked manager who explained it all to dumbfounded journalists in typically avuncular fashion at around 3pm on 6th May 2018. There had never been a more buoyant mood in the Cardiff City Stadium press conference room.

The size of the media pack following Warnock's team had grown by the week at the climax of that 2017/18 season. A year earlier, as Warnock saw out an unremarkable mid-table season – which was remarkable in its own way (but more on that later) – there had been just three journalists at one press conference at the Vale Resort Hotel in Pontyclun, on Cardiff's outskirts.

I was one of the lucky trio. Now, Warnock was the centre of the universe, happily providing chapter and verse to the country's broadcast, print and online media – who were lapping it up. The next day's headlines would write themselves, even though Warnock's responses always made good copy. His reaction to Natalie's phone call was somehow a microcosm of the 18-month tenure that had gone before. Always relatable, always human, usually humorous.

Moments before, Warnock had stood in the Cardiff City Stadium Grandstand, looking out onto a sea of blue that had descended on the green turf. Shirts, scarves, flags, flares; pertinently a packed stadium of fans wearing the blue colours in which Cardiff City belong.

Midfielder Joe Ralls was mobbed at the final whistle, captain Sean Morrison danced to the tune of the triumphant Canton Stand's songs, owner Vincent Tan was hoisted onto the shoulders of fans. Bedlam.

It hadn't always been this way.

Not even during Cardiff's previous (and only other) promotion to the Premier League, which had been achieved with an identical result, 0-0 at home to Charlton Athletic. Sure, there was joy and emotion on that night in April 2013, but it will always be tarnished in the minds of supporters because red was the colour. Owner Vincent Tan's controversial decision to rebrand the Bluebirds was not reversed until the early months of 2015.

It wasn't just the blue colours that made 2018 more special, though. There was something about Warnock. The way he spoke. His honesty. His passion. The way he'd tease the Canton after a victory by circling his fist before punching the air, anticipating the roar. The way he'd harangue officials for something as small as a throw-in this way or that. The way his team played, with pace and fearlessness. The way he and his players seemed to care more than the rest.

It was evident from the first day of the Warnock regime, back in October 2016, that this would be a marriage made in heaven. His opening salvo, in the same Cardiff City Stadium press conference room, hit all the right notes with supporters.

"My kind of club. My kind of people."

It wasn't intended as a media-friendly soundbite. Yet Warnock's words always made the back page, for good or bad, and these words ended up on the side of the stadium itself. Everything felt right from the moment he was unveiled as manager.

"I've always liked it here," said a smiling Warnock on

5th October. "Everywhere I go I get stick but I've always had good banter with the Cardiff people.

"They're my type of crowd – blood and guts and all that, which I like – and I know that if I can get it right for them, they'll get behind me."

From that first day to the glorious scenes of May 2018, you could not ignore Neil Warnock's Cardiff City.

I happened to be present for both promotions. When Malky Mackay's 'red' Bluebirds went up, I was working in a food kiosk serving the away fans, an ideal part-time job for a football fan like myself while studying at Cardiff University.

It was deserted in my section after the final whistle, as nonplussed Charlton fans had made their way home, but the noise of the celebrations was unmistakable. It was nothing like I'd experienced before. I ran out into the stands to see what the fuss was about.

Six years later, I was in the aforementioned press conference, having trained to be a journalist and earned a job at *WalesOnline*. I had the pleasure of following Warnock's Cardiff the length and breadth of the country that 2017/18 season – and the following year in the Premier League. And although the promotion seems an apt place to begin and end, the Warnock-Cardiff story isn't a fairytale. Maybe it felt like one on that night when the sun had finally set on the Bluebirds' greatest day, the night Sol Bamba, Junior Hoilett and Sean Morrison (plus me and my wide-eyed Cardiff-supporting friend Simon Edwards) partied in Cardiff's Tiger Tiger nightclub. But there would be as many lows as highs, especially in the following top-flight campaign.

It's a story I felt I needed to tell. Warnock, during his time in the Welsh capital, was a figure you couldn't ignore. And he made Cardiff, a football team sometimes overlooked by the wider rugby-loving Welsh public, the centrepiece of the nation.

His work was derided as old-school, old-fashioned and prehistoric from those outside the bubble. But inside we – even as impartial journalists – always believed. He made us believe.

We listened dutifully every week at the Vale Hotel as Warnock spoke, usually about being backed into a corner, about his limited budget, his "great group of lads", the size of the challenge ahead and we lapped it up. It was hard to remain impartial as the story grew and Cardiff marched on. Even the most professional journalist would have been sucked in.

So this is the story that shouldn't have happened. The

tale of the ultimate underdog? You could call it that. And Warnock – who has been kind enough to lend his contributions to this book – would agree.

It's probably more appropriate to swerve the hyperbole and say simply that this is the story of a football club that went on an unfathomable journey. The ultimate rollercoaster.

I hope you enjoy reliving it with me.

Dominic Booth

CHAPTER ONE

Picking Up The Pieces

Fragments. Everywhere.

That's how Neil Warnock described the scene that laid before him at Cardiff City in October 2016 when, following a phone call from chairman Mehmet Dalman, he swiftly accepted the job by signing his name on a napkin.

It had been a rough time for Cardiff since their relegation from the Premier League in May 2014.

Even setting aside the controversial 2012 rebrand from their traditional blue colours to the red that owner Vincent Tan was convinced would bring success – and the subsequent reversal of that decision – it had been a rough time.

It had been a rough time because they had criminally

overspent after finding themselves in the Premier League for the first time in their history. An ugly row between promotion-winning manager Malky Mackay and Tan also left its mark, emotionally and financially.

Legally too, as Tan pursued Mackay in the courts when the former boss was stung for exchanging offensive text messages with the club's former head of recruitment, Iain Moody.

It had been a rough time because the club's Mackay replacement, Ole Gunnar Solskjaer, had looked out of his depth, having been appointed on the back of a league title win with Norwegian side Molde – and his history as a Premier League legend with Manchester United – as well as a gut feeling from Dalman.

It continued to be rough in the era of Russell Slade, the former Leyton Orient manager who was viewed as a steady hand on the tiller following Solskjaer's dismissal in September 2014. Slade had it tough when Cardiff were back in the Championship and a major cost-cutting operation was under way.

Even when Tan was persuaded to swap the colours back to blue in February 2015, the crowds wouldn't flock back to Cardiff City Stadium. The relationship was beyond repair, many said. Slade's football was perceived as dull and his task to slash the club's bloated wage bill resulted in a less-than exciting squad.

"Cardiff City were at the point where the whole philosophy had gone out of the window – there was no philosophy," says Bluebirds legend and former Wales striker Nathan Blake.

"It wasn't something the owners would have even thought about when they took over the business, from how they saw it.

"Lots of owners think, 'I'll just buy a football club, buy some players and get a manager and we'll win!' If only it was that easy."

It wasn't. When a push for the play-offs fell short in spring 2016, the decision was made to move Slade upstairs. He accepted a role as head of football, as a young and exciting new coach, Paul Trollope, was given the manager's job.

Trollope had been part of Wales' backroom staff during their thrilling run to the Euro 2016 semi-finals and vowed to bring 'the Wales Way' to the nation's capital city club. He brought Euro 2016 squad members Jazz Richards and Emyr Huws to Cardiff among his first signings and promised to replicate Chris Coleman's wing-back system that had surprised Europe's behemoths in France that summer. And despite his lack of experience in management – having only a stint at Bristol Rovers that ended in 2010 to fall back upon – there was guarded optimism among Bluebirds fans that this could be the start of something.

Blake had his doubts, however, and he was soon proven right as the move sent Cardiff even further backwards.

"Trollope had been at Bristol Rovers before Cardiff," he says. "Did okay there – below average probably, you'd say. But he was never going to be the right answer in a million years.

"What did the club, the chairman and board of directors see in Paul Trollope and how he could take the club to the next level? How did he fit into your strategy?"

Just as Solskjaer's naivety had been to his detriment, and Slade was punished for his own conservatism, Trollope was quickly found out and Cardiff fans were left craving for a return to the days of Malky Mackay, Davie Jones or legendary 1990s manager Eddie May. Even Mackay, while successful, was anathema in the minds of the club's hierarchy and his tenure in any case had been soured by the red-shirted, hollow celebrations.

As Blake said, Trollope wasn't up to it, either. His 12 games in charge yielded just two wins. Key pillars of the side, like Icelander Aron Gunnarsson, were ostracised. Others were shoehorned into a system that clearly wasn't working.

By the time of Trollope's nadir, a 2-0 defeat at Burton Albion, Slade was already long gone from his executive role. He had been lured back into management with Charlton Athletic.

Trollope was on his own in every sense. The club's new structure and new identity were in tatters within weeks and the fanbase was as disparate as in those dark days when red reigned supreme.

Warnock, who had left Rotherham in that 2016 summer after pulling off the most miraculous escape, saw it all unfold from the outside.

"I'd watched the previous game before I took over and they got well beaten 2-0 at Burton," Warnock says.

"Joe Ralls was a left-winger in that game! I knew they'd got some good players. I just felt I could do something with this lot. Not just with the team, they'd had all the problems with the colour change and everything else, and it was a fragmented club."

If Warnock was convinced he would be the right man, then Dalman, immediately after sacking Trollope on 4th October, knew it too.

The Turkish-Cypriot acts as the conduit between Cardiff's managers and the omnipotent Tan. The owner received criticism in spades following the rebrand but Dalman was – and remained – his shield. In the years since, Tan has been more of an absent owner, picking his moments to attend matches and rarely agreeing to interviews.

Dalman's role was less chairman, more mediator. His background is in investment banking, with a lifelong love of football, and this blend of knowledge had seen him act as an adviser to the Glazer family when completing their takeover of Manchester United in 2005.

He is a shrewd and composed negotiator and his prudence was never more necessary than during the Warnock years.

Dalman's first challenge, after identifying Warnock as the No.1 candidate for the role – "he was the obvious choice" according to Blake – was to persuade the Yorkshireman to accept the job.

Despite being a wanted man after his Rotherham heroics, Warnock, approaching his 68th birthday, remained out of work. But he was certainly on the radar of owners looking to make an early season change. Derby chairman Mel Morris was on the prowl for a new manager having suspended Nigel Pearson amid a training ground bust-up and had contacted Warnock.

"It was funny because I was in Scotland when he [Dalman] called me from London," Warnock recalls. "He said, 'Can we meet?' and I said, 'Yeah I'll fly down tomorrow'.

"So I flew down and met him. He knew about Derby's interest, someone had told him."

The attraction for Warnock was the challenge of turning Cardiff's fortunes around. The Bluebirds were second from bottom, a similar position to the one the veteran manager had inherited when taking over Rotherham in February that year – 22nd in the Championship, having lost eight of their past 12 league matches before Warnock's appointment.

And although keeping the South Yorkshire side in the Championship was a miracle in its own right, the difference was Cardiff were a bigger club with greater potential. Warnock could smell the prospect of an eighth promotion as a manager, which would be an English league record if he got it. And it was only the start of October. Plenty of time to turn this lot around, Warnock thought.

The Dalman factor made a difference, too.

"We met at this London gentlemen's club and had a bite of breakfast and as I was talking to him I got these feelings, which you do as a manager," says Warnock.

"Straight away I was relaxed, I was confident and I just had a trust in him, from the first minute I set eyes on him. I thought, 'Yeah I can work for you'. And then he started talking about Cardiff.

"We talked about it and within about half an hour I said to him, 'I'll take the job, Mehmet'. We didn't talk about money. He said he'd have to speak to Vincent and see about the finances and things. So off he went [on the phone] for about 10 minutes. And he came back in, we talked finances and I told him the situation with me."

Warnock hadn't taken a job in August, before the Championship season had begun, despite interest from Blackburn and Nottingham Forest. He had also rejected a new contract at Rotherham as he felt – with a new lease of life for management after what he had achieved, safety – that the top of the Championship was calling again.

"I just wanted a chance at a promotion and it would've been wrong to stay at Rotherham for a promotion, as I would have been staying for the money," adds Warnock of his conversations with the South Yorkshire club's chairman Tony Stewart that summer.

"And I wanted to wait for a job where I thought I could get a promotion and that was how we left it.

"But that belief was amazing. And I knew that I'd still got it in me. To turn that club around and see the fans at the end... I knew I could do that. Rotherham was amazing for me. Rotherham is the reason why I did what I did at Cardiff."

Warnock's word, at that gentlemen's club in London, wasn't quite enough for Dalman and Tan. After hiring the wrong man in Trollope, they didn't want to lose the right man in Warnock.

A contract had to be signed, with the timing ideal during the second international break of the season. Warnock had also received contact from Aston Villa, who had just sacked Roberto Di Matteo and were looking for a promotion specialist of their own.

Warnock remembers: "Mehmet said, 'We want you to sign something' because obviously he was aware of Derby. I spoke to a few clubs including Blackburn and Forest but I said, 'No, I'll just shake your hand, that's my signature Mehmet'.

"I said this is my hand, that I trusted him and I wouldn't be going anywhere else. I said, 'I'll be in charge of the next game against Bristol City at home'.

"He was desperate for me to sign something though, so I said, 'Tell you what, I'll sign that' – and got a serviette off the table and signed that."

* * * *

There is an illuminating documentary made by Mat Hodgson that charts a tumultuous time at Queens Park Rangers between 2007 and 2011. It covers the period from the club's takeover by a consortium of billionaires, headed up by Formula One business magnates Bernie Ecclestone and Flavio Briatore and also including Alejandro Agag, Lakshmi Mittal and Amit Bhatia, to their promotion to the Premier League at the climax of the 2010/11 season, as champions.

It is fittingly named *The Four Year Plan*, ultimately an ironic title taken from Briatore's mission statement when acquiring the club. The aim was to transform QPR and build them into an established Premier League team within four years. Thereafter lay even loftier ambitions about becoming the best team in London and even bringing Champions League football to Loftus Road.

The documentary is a remarkable insight into the

boardroom at an aspirational Championship club. Its highlights are the conversations between the powerbrokers, showing how their astonishing knee-jerk decisions came about. From the chaos when Briatore was running the show, to the rather more considered leadership of Bhatia.

What also shines out like a beacon is the impact of Neil Warnock. Brought from Crystal Palace to replace Mick Harford in March 2010 after years of mismanagement and fractures within the club's hierarchy and fanbase, he proves a unifying figure.

Despite all that went before – he became their fifth manager of the 2009/10 season and their ninth in less than three years – Warnock managed to work through the turbulence, bring dressing room, boardroom and terraces together and win promotion. He's still remembered as a hero among QPR fans and is warmly welcomed on every visit back to Loftus Road to this day.

It would be simplistic and unfair to suggest that what happened at Cardiff pre-Warnock is identical to those seasons in the first half of *The Four Year Plan*, but the parallels are stark.

A fragmented club, destabilised at the top and apathetic in the stands, waiting for impending relegation to League

One and harbouring unfulfilled dreams of the top flight. It shows how unrealistic and idealistic aims of winning promotion on a shoestring budget will never come to fruition, unless, it seems, Neil Warnock is in charge of your club with little recent history of success.

Yet in both QPR and Cardiff's cases, the charismatic leadership of one man – able to manage both upwards and downwards – allowed the football to flourish.

And when results begin to come good, suddenly you find that tensions ease and everyone remembers life working at a football club can be fun.

When Warnock got that call from Mehmet Dalman in October 2016, it appeared to be the perfect storm, as it had been at QPR. He had been particularly annoyed at some clubs' decisions to go with younger, more fashionable or cheaper options in the dugout, as owners up and down the land went crazy in an ill-advised quest to ape Pep Guardiola's Barcelona tactics in the hurly-burly of the Championship.

Warnock waited for Cardiff and he wouldn't be playing tiki-taka. He would do it his way.

"I remember speaking to Blackburn and they quibbled about the wages I wanted at one stage and I think they appointed Owen Coyle, who was obviously a cheaper option," says Warnock. "But I do believe in fate and I think things happen for a reason."

Fate brought Cardiff and Warnock together, in his view, and ensured his trusted lieutenants Kevin Blackwell and Ronnie Jepson would come as part of the package, as they had done at Rotherham as assistant and first-team manager respectively. Blackwell had been a manager outright at Leeds, Luton, Sheffield United and Bury in his time while Jepson first played under Warnock at Huddersfield in 1993 and had worked under him at various clubs.

Glen Williams, Cardiff City correspondent for *WalesOnline*, describes the situation appropriately. "It was an SOS call from the club and he took them from the bottom end of the Championship to the Premier League in 18 months. Through sheer togetherness and team spirit as well – and how rare is that?"

"For the short-term fix, which sometimes you plan for, he was a great choice," says Nathan Blake.

"You plan for the short, medium and long-term in football. And with no philosophy to fall back on, you're drifting and going nowhere fast, heading towards a relegation battle.

"A lot of players weren't happy with how the situation

was and in my opinion Cardiff were drifting towards League One.

"Neil shone out like a beacon of light because he'd done it before. And not only had he saved clubs, but he'd won promotion. So he was ticking both boxes – if by some minor miracle he got Cardiff promoted."

The match was made, and at his first press conference Warnock remembered his visits as an opposition manager to Cardiff's old Ninian Park ground – their home until Cardiff City Stadium was completed in 2009 – and his jokes with locals about why he'd never been asked to manage the Bluebirds.

"I loved the fans at the old Ninian Park, it was my kind of place," says Warnock.

"When I got promoted with QPR, the game at Ninian Park with [Jay] Bothroyd and [Craig] Bellamy, the atmosphere that afternoon was quite unbelievable.

"Mick Jones was my assistant then and I used to say to Mick, 'Wow, you could do something with this lot, couldn't you?' They're like a Yorkshire mentality, the Cardiff fans, us against the world and I like that. Let's show 'em."

It was simply assumed that one day Warnock would find himself in the City hotseat. Fate?

Warnock would suggest as much upon his appointment. "All blood and guts, which I like," he said of that Welsh fighting spirit that appealed so much.

Warnock's arrival felt like panacea for supporters who had quickly become despondent that autumn after the usual pre-season dreams of promotion.

It was simply never going to happen playing the 'Wales Way' with the inexperienced Trollope.

The beleaguered manager had made a rod for his own back: jettisoning the influential midfielder Aron Gunnarsson, playing ageing Rickie Lambert up front and sidelining his only pace merchant Kadeem Harris on the right at wing-back. And Ralls on the left of midfield, of course.

Cardiff fans made their feelings clear on that dreadful day at Burton, a Staffordshire town on the River Trent known more for brewing beer than its football team.

There was certainly an unsavoury atmosphere brewing among the Bluebirds supporters that day. "Sacked in the morning," they chanted to their own manager.

"I can understand it," Trollope told reporters at the Pirelli Stadium.

"I can understand the frustration, I'm frustrated in myself and the position we're in, because it's not where we should be and it's not where we want to be. They pay their money and they sing what they sing, but we're working hard, the international break affords us some time to hopefully improve."

But it was inevitable that the international break would bring about nothing but Trollope's demise. Fans couldn't take any more and the emergency call to Warnock was made and answered in that London meeting.

Just as the veteran manager had followed where others – Iain Dowie, Paulo Sousa and Jim Magilton – had failed at QPR, he felt he was destined to succeed at Cardiff, despite the disastrous Trollope tenure.

"Very similar," says Warnock on the two jobs.

"The only thing about Cardiff in comparison to QPR was I had Mehmet. It would have been very difficult to do what I did at Cardiff without Mehmet.

"At QPR I had two really powerful men in Bernie and Flavio. Flavio in particular thought he was the best manager. He'd tell me who to pick and try to tell poor old Gianni Paladini [former QPR chairman]. It was a different breed in that respect but I had the same problems."

So the template was there and Warnock had the right man in Dalman by his side.

He didn't even need a fancy mission statement, or anything like four years, to work his magic. Just like at QPR, around 18 months and one full season at the helm would do the trick.

CHAPTER TWO

Moulding The Squad

Sol Bamba and Junior Hoilett waited. They waited a long time. For established Championship players, aged 31 and 26 respectively, to go without employment or payment for three months is almost unheard of in the modern era.

And when Hoilett became Warnock's first signing at Cardiff on 10th October, five days after the manager's arrival, it was reported that the winger was "understood to have been waiting for a Premier League offer after leaving QPR following the expiration of his contract in the summer".

It wasn't quite true, even if the Canadian winger did have Premier League pedigree with Blackburn as well as Warnock's old club the Rs. And Hoilett did see his long-term future in the top flight. But the truth was both he and Bamba waited for Warnock, having been earmarked as ideal signings for the veteran manager. No matter which club, he wanted them and they wanted him.

Bamba, whose career had been nomadic to this point, departed Leeds United by mutual consent in August despite being their club captain and starting the first two games of the season under Garry Monk. But Monk had plans to shake up the squad at Elland Road and Bamba was the fall guy.

"I spoke with Sol and I told him that I didn't think it was a good situation for him not being in the squad, that it wouldn't be a healthy situation," Monk told the *Yorkshire Evening Post*.

"I asked the club to find a solution and he understood that. They came to an agreement."

That meant three months in the wilderness for Bamba, who had previously had spells in Scotland, Turkey and Italy as well as in the Championship and had represented his parents' nation, Ivory Coast, at the 2010 World Cup. But the Paris-raised centre-back, who speaks with a unique accent that blends his French upbringing with a Scottish lilt – from five years at Hibernian and Dunfermine Athletic – wasn't concerned.

He knew which manager he would next work alongside.

He had met Warnock way back in 2012 and struck up an instant rapport.

"I left Leeds and he told me, 'Don't sign for anyone yet, just wait for me, I'll have a club soon'," reveals Bamba, who briefly trained with former manager Nigel Pearson at Derby in September 2016, before agreeing a free transfer to Cardiff on 11th October, a day after Hoilett had signed.

"He knew it was a big gamble for me because of my family and not getting paid, but he guaranteed me he'd get a club and take me.

"One minute he told me we were going to Aston Villa, then the next day he said we were going to Derby, then Nottingham Forest. Every day it was a different club!

"But he was pleased I waited for him and I think it showed him a lot about me. Because I had a family, a mortgage, bills to pay, and I had a few options to go back to France and offers from a few clubs in England.

"But from that moment on, we had a strong relationship and as soon as we got to that first game, he told me, 'Just cut out the silly mistakes – play simple and everything's going to be okay'."

Bamba and Warnock's relationship began, funnily enough, at Elland Road on 28th April 2012 with Bamba playing for Leicester and Warnock in charge of Leeds. Straight away Warnock saw a player he could mould and a personality that was striking similar to his own: an affable, loud leader.

"Me and the gaffer, I've said it a thousand times, we were dying to work with each other for a very long time," says Bamba, recalling that Leeds versus Leicester game when Warnock made a beeline for the centre-back after the game.

"He ran onto the pitch towards me and said, 'You need to come and play for me'.

"And I was a bit shocked, I was obviously shaking hands with other players and I wanted to thank the Leicester fans as it was the last day of the season. He said, 'If you play for me, you'll be a better player. I'll make you into a Premier League player.'

"I knew the guy from reputation, I knew some guys who'd worked with him and said only good things. But I was shocked for him to come and do that at the end of the game.

"He actually had an argument with Nigel Pearson, who was annoyed. I remember seeing Pearson in the tunnel waiting for Warnock and they started arguing in front of the dressing room.

"Pearson was like, 'You can't go up to my players like that' and Warnock said, 'I don't care, he's a good player'.

"That sums the gaffer up, when he wants something he'll do everything he can to go and get it. And it stuck with me, to be fair. I thought, 'I've got to work with that guy at some point'."

Hoilett, meanwhile, had already worked with Warnock before, briefly, at QPR in the manager's second stint at Loftus Road. Warnock had been brought back to the West London club as a caretaker manager in 2015 and he immediately reinstated Hoilett – who had been marginalised and training with the Under-18s – to the Rs' first team. He rated the winger very highly and knew he could shine in the Championship.

In, too, came Kieran Richardson and Marouane Chamakh, on free transfers, though these were more on a whim – a gut feeling from Warnock that the squad needed an almighty shake-up. Freebies were the only transfers he was allowed until January.

"They weren't quite as effective as Sol or Junior but I just wanted to get a few numbers in to change it up, because they were in a pretty dire situation really," Warnock admits. Both players left within a few months.

And Bamba wasn't the finished article until Warnock

got down to work with him. The Ivorian had a tendency to over-elaborate in defence but his new manager, who would later tell the press that Bamba wanted to play like German legend Franz Beckenbauer, gave the centre-back some stern instructions from the very first day in South Wales.

Bamba says: "I remember when I met him before I signed for Cardiff, we were at the Vale Hotel and he said, 'I saw you play for years and you've got so much potential, but you're always getting away with murder because you're always smiling'.

"'The managers are too nice to you. Someone needs to have a go at you every now and then'."

* * * *

Four players had been signed before Warnock's Cardiff City had even kicked a ball, but the squad-building process would have to continue in January, when the window officially opened and Warnock was already plotting the following season's path to promotion.

The on-loan capture of goalkeeper Allan McGregor from Hull City until the end of the season was a necessary short-term deal, however, with Warnock unhappy with his existing No.1 option in goal, Ben Amos. He needed someone solid between the posts.

Cardiff did lodge an unsuccessful £200,000 bid for Walsall's Neil Etheridge in January 2017. The Midlands club wanted £350,000, so Warnock decided to wait until the summer, when he could sign Etheridge on a free. Nothing ventured, nothing gained. He would get his man in the end.

The only permanent addition Cardiff made in January 2017 was the quietly significant arrival of Greg Halford, a stalwart of Warnock's relegation-defying Rotherham side the previous season. Halford was a Swiss army knife footballer, willing and able to do any job his manager asked of him.

He too was a veteran of the leagues, having represented Sunderland, Nottingham Forest, Portsmouth, Sheffield United and Wolves and had played in virtually every outfield position on the pitch at one stage or another. But he'd turned down Warnock's advances while at Colchester in 2006/07 and regretted it.

Of all the managers Halford played under, it was Warnock who lit the flame in him when they eventually paired up at Rotherham. And like Bamba and Hoilett,

Halford was desperate to join the manager's Bluebirds revolution.

"I think he brought me to Cardiff because of what I was able to achieve at Rotherham, that massive turnaround that we had at the bottom of the league where we flipped an 11-point gap from relegation to safety," he says.

"He bought me as one of the main parts that could help do that job and obviously with my versatility coming into the club, he felt that was an asset.

"I was good friends with Kevin Blackwell, who was my manager at Sheffield United and he put in a good word for me. It happened really quickly. Rotherham wanted me off the wage bill and Neil wanted to take me at Cardiff as soon as he could.

"He has this reputation of bringing out the best in the players he has. And if you do well for him, he will look after you.

"There's been numerous players that have followed him to clubs because they have a good rapport with him and they think he's the only man to get the best from them. I think if we'd crossed paths earlier then my career could have headed in a different direction."

But it wasn't just about signing players for a promotion push. Warnock knew there was a considerable mess to sort out in the immediate term and he would have to made some ruthless decisions with players like Rickie Lambert and Peter Whittingham, who were key men under Trollope but unable to play the high-octane, up-and-at-em football that Warnock knew would work in the Championship.

There was also the small matter of clinching the results to guide the Bluebirds up the table and away from danger.

As he assessed the squad in that first week at the Vale Resort, Cardiff's training ground, Warnock still wasn't too worried about the threat of relegation to League One. With Bamba and Hoilett in tow and a decent existing squad, he saw plenty of quality.

"The likes of Mozza [Sean Morrison], [Lee] Peltier I knew, and Joe Ralls who I'd quite liked as a player – not on the left-wing, mind," says Warnock.

"I didn't think there were enough goals in them. There were some lads, looking at the squad, who I knew we'd have to change. And I did that at the end of the season. But we got the dressing room together and then it was just that the fans trusted me from day one."

And the players did too. They were imbued with a new energy that had been draining out of them before Warnock's arrival.

"The boys trained really well all week and it was like trying to rein them in really – they were that aggressive and everyone wanted to please me," says Warnock. "It was just channelling that into one goal."

The one goal was Bristol City, a home match under Cardiff City Stadium's Friday night lights on 14th October. The press excitably billed it as a battle between Warnock and Bristol City manager Lee Johnson, as the two had exchanged a few choice words in the past. But in reality it was Cardiff and Warnock against the world and he geared that first week at the club towards beating the Bluebirds' Severnside rivals.

"It took off from there really. The lads thought we could beat anybody. They were like little boys, really. They needed guidance. They'd just gone astray, they'd gone off the rails a little bit and it was like going back to school. They needed telling. They were all good players – because they wouldn't be there if they weren't.

"I told them they were [at Cardiff] for a reason but they'd stopped doing what they were good at. The main thing for me was for them to enjoy it, for them to smile."

There would be plenty of reasons to smile straight away.

CHAPTER THREE

The First Game

Cardiff City 2-1 Bristol City, 14th October 2016
Cardiff (4-3-3): Amos; Peltier, Morrison, Bamba, Bennett; Gunnarsson, Whittingham (Immers, 65), Ralls; Hoilett (Harris, 72), Noone, Lambert (Pilkington, 84).
Subs not used: Wilson, Manga, Richardson, Chamakh.
Bristol City (4-2-3-1): Fielding; Little, Flint, Magnusson, Bryan; O'Neil, Pack (Reid, 55); Paterson (Wilbraham, 55), Tomlin, Freeman; Abraham (O'Dowda, 80).
Subs not used: O'Donnell, Golbourne, Brownhill, Moore.
Cardiff goals: Whittingham (pen, 25), Bamba (67).
Bristol City goal: Tomlin (69).

Just as Warnock remembers, Cardiff City trained superbly in the week leading up to Friday night's Severnside derby, the Wales versus England battle between the two teams either side of the Severn Estuary. In fact, the squad felt that the training was better than at any time during Paul Trollope's spell at the club.

The situation equated to the perfect storm: a new manager, a game against the club's nearest rivals and even the Sky Sports cameras would be at Cardiff City Stadium, so the Bluebirds players could prove to the nation they weren't relegation fodder, and that the table was lying.

Warnock knew the conditions would favour his approach, of course, and had spoken like an excited child at his official unveiling, which had doubled up as a pre-match press conference. He couldn't wait for the thrill of managing the Bluebirds for the first time.

"I suppose if I lost that feeling I'd be in trouble," Warnock reflected, obviously reinvigorated from his experience at Rotherham. "Even when I was going to speak to Cardiff, when I was travelling down, I was excited. I don't think my mate could shut me up."

Yet despite the appointment and Warnock's dream of a record eighth promotion, the column inches before the match were dominated by his beef with Bristol City boss Lee Johnson.

Before Warnock's Rotherham were due to meet the Robins in April, Johnson outlined his intention to "win the match, whether we do it through aggression, good football or intimidation" – comments that didn't please Warnock. After a feisty 1-1 draw, he called Johnson "a disgrace" and suggested the Bristol City manager had motivated the Rotherham players: "I didn't have to do a teamtalk."

He likened Johnson's words to those of the Bristol City manager's father, Gary, with whom Warnock had quarrelled in the past. "Like father, like son," he said.

While the press stoked that particular fire, Warnock was calm. His Cardiff players were getting all the motivation they needed, thanks to his man-management skills and the training methods of assistants Ronnie Jepson and Kevin Blackwell.

Warnock even found time to flatter Johnson in his press conference, referencing the fact that – like Warnock – the Bristol City boss had recently been linked with the vacant Aston Villa job.

But Cardiff manager's relationship with Bristol City, in general, had long been strained – to the point where he'd once joked that when he died he would want a minute's booing at Ashton Gate rather than silence or applause. It was meant tongue-in-cheek – and was a classic Warnock one-liner – but the choice of club was carefully considered.

"When I go to Bristol City I do get stick," he added before the Friday night contest. "I thought it was a little bit over the top prior to the [Rotherham] game, but I think you're going to get that sort of thing when you're a manager. I haven't spoken to him since, though.

"We're not on each other's Christmas card lists. He was linked with Aston Villa last week, wasn't he? So he's doing something right."

Despite the ambitious football Johnson was determined to play with Bristol City, the game itself was poor, lacking in quality. But that's just the way Warnock wanted it.

From the moment right-back Lee Peltier launched the ball forward from kick off, Cardiff's plan was clear: to spoil the visitors' attempts to play possession football.

Under Trollope Cardiff had been a poor imitation of teams like Bristol City, who were riding high in the Championship at the time thanks to their free-flowing approach. And victory in the Welsh capital could have sent them second in the table.

Under Warnock, the Bluebirds would be the polar opposite of a possession team, despite the fact that Lee Tomlin, Aden Flint, Marlon Pack and Bobby Reid (later Decordova-Reid, after changing his name via deed poll) – who all featured for Bristol City that October night in

2016 – would later sign for Cardiff. The early stages were scruffy – typified by a spell of 11 consecutive headers around the nine-minute mark – but debutant Sol Bamba showed no signs of rustiness after two months out of the game. He was desperate to repay Warnock's faith in him with a man of the match performance.

"The first game was massive," says Bamba, looking back. "It was a big change for the lads when the gaffer and I arrived, but I knew some of the lads from playing against them or playing with them.

"He was a breath of fresh air, but it's a results business and the fact we won that first game was massive. It sent a message to the squad, to the fans, to the media.

"And the fact I had a good game and scored a goal really helped, because when I came in to be really honest I don't think Cardiff needed a central defender.

"They had plenty of defenders on the books: they had Bruno Manga, Matthew Connolly and obviously Sean Morrison as well."

Bamba was selected ahead of Manga and Connolly that night and his partnership with Morrison proved rock solid, as they nullified the threat of teenage Chelsea loanee Tammy Abraham, playing up front for the visitors. Abraham would finish the season with a goal tally of 26 in all competitions, but he barely got a kick out of Bamba and Morrison.

Warnock, in a 90-minute period, had discovered the foundations on which his Bluebirds would be built; the perfect combination in central defence.

Bamba adds: "Neil didn't necessarily need another body in there, but he said to me over the years that my character and my spirit was needed in the dressing room.

"Neil said, 'I know you'll come in with a smile on your face, with positivity, and that's what's needed'."

Cardiff didn't create much but the stadium erupted after 24 minutes when Peter Whittingham slotted home the opener from the penalty spot, after a clear foul from Joe Bryan on Craig Noone in the box.

The Welsh side continued to defend manfully, with Aron Gunnarsson particularly combative and competitive on his return to the side, until Bamba made it 2-0 on 67 minutes. It came, perhaps inevitably, from a set-piece.

Joe Ralls' whipped delivery found the head of Rickie Lambert who nodded onto the crossbar, before Bamba won the race for the loose ball and stabbed home. Cue joyous celebrations and a trademark Bamba smile as he raced away to celebrate.

Tomlin then caught Ben Amos on his heels with a

swift response to reduce the visitors' arrears to 2-1, but thereafter Cardiff saw out the victory thanks to their determined defence. Luke Freeman and Reid spurned big chances to level an equal contest, but Cardiff's sheer desire seemed to have played a big part in the win.

Despite the performances of captain Morrison and midfield general Gunnarson, the headline act had been Bamba, as well as Warnock of course. The two of them had captured the imagination of the Cardiff public in just one game.

For supporters it was just pleasing to see the Bluebirds play with fire and passion – two words that remained on their club's crest – for the first time in months.

Bamba was indeed named man of the match for his tremendous work in both boxes and his influential display was a sign of things to come for Cardiff fans. Warnock claimed after the game that Bamba had "wasted his career at times [doing] nutmegs and all sorts of things in the last five years – he thinks he's Beckenbauer".

It was a comment meant in jest, yet Leeds had been happy to see Bamba leave for that very reason. For Warnock it was about channelling Bamba's best traits on the pitch and to inspire performances like the one against Bristol City.

"Leeds fans always said Sol was an accident waiting to happen," says Warnock. "But in training I told him, 'Be a defender first'.

"I still say that now when I see some of these passing it out from the back and some of the goals they concede. Defenders have got to be defenders first and foremost and with Sol I didn't want him to get over-complacent and I thought he and Mozza were magnificent for us."

The victory would be Warnock's base camp at Cardiff City; the game that built all the early momentum and allowed them to climb the league, but also the place to which he'd return when times were tough.

There remained, however, a huge amount of work to do and four players in the starting XI that night – Amos, Whittingham, Lambert and Noone – would depart in the summer of 2017.

Yet others like Gunnarsson, Morrison and Ralls had been re-energised and were ready to play a full part for their new manager. Joe Bennett had been injured under Trollope but made his Cardiff debut against Bristol City and looked a class act at left-back. Goals and creativity would be an issue but energy and work rate had been enough on this occasion.

"To see a team of lads die for me, I can't ask any more," Warnock told reporters immediately after the game. "We've got limitations, I know we have, but those lads gave everything."

Those limitations would be ironed out in time, but three points to clamber out of the Championship bottom three and set the Bluebirds on course for comfortable survival was plenty to savour in the short-term.

The first steps of the mountain had been climbed.

CHAPTER FOUR

Managing Up
And Down

When people in football realised Cardiff City would be pairing Vincent Tan with Neil Warnock, they predicted fireworks.

Falling out with owners had been a penchant of Warnock's over the years, with the veteran manager rightly particular about the kind of men he can and cannot work for. The 'disputes' section of his Wikipedia page is famously lengthy and, as well as former players, managers and referees (plus Sheffield United supporting actor Sean Bean), it includes former chairmen, chief executives and owners.

But perhaps the media hadn't seen *The Four Year Plan*, or gleaned anything from Warnock's exemplary dealings with the volatile Queens Park Rangers board years before. He could toe the line when he needed to, even when under undue pressure.

Flavio Briatore had once wanted to sack Warnock when his QPR side – on the brink of promotion – suffered a surprise defeat to Scunthorpe in April 2011. They only needed three wins from six more games to become a Premier League side but the ignominy of a crushing defeat to the Championship's bottom club had the owners reaching for the panic button.

"I remember at Easter we lost 4-1 at Scunthorpe and I had Flavio on the phone saying, 'The manager will have to go, he doesn't know what he's doing'," Warnock recalls.

"And I told Bernie Ecclestone, 'Don't listen to what Flavio is saying, just trust me'. Bernie said, 'I would never listen to Flavio, I do trust you'."

In his 2013 book *Gaffer*, Warnock mused on his employers' lack of football understanding, an issue he has regularly encountered when dealing with chairmen and owners.

He added: "I'm thinking, 'I know they don't understand football but does anybody want a result like that'? You don't plan for results like that. I said, 'Bernie, you've got to leave it with me, let me deal with it'."

Thankfully for Cardiff City, Warnock had an owner who – despite his critics – let the manager get on with his job. Most of the time.

Vincent Tan had been heavily criticised for his decision, in June 2012, to change the club's iconic blue colours to red, with a new dragon crest replacing the traditional bluebird.

The decision was borne out of discussions between the Malaysian owner and fellow countryman and Cardiff investor Dato Chan Tien Ghee, known as TG, and a desire to bring the traditional colours and symbols of Malaysia and Wales to the home shirts of the capital's football club.

TG, who had initially persuaded Tan to buy into the club in 2010, cited "a symbolic fusion with Asia which will allow us to fly the Welsh flag on behalf of Cardiff wherever we go".

It was a disastrous move, leaving Bluebirds fans furious, believing their club had become the play-thing of an aloof and uncaring owner who did not understand football. There followed years of ill-feeling between supporters and Tan, amid stories that the owner was meddling in footballing matters.

It opened up gaping wounds that would take years to

heal. Tan's fall-out and the subsequent sacking of popular manager Malky Mackay was just the tip of the iceberg for many fans, who had caught the public's attention at Liverpool's Anfield ground in December 2013 when chanting 'Don't sack Mackay' on repeat.

Mackay was sacked, of course. And following Cardiff's 2014 relegation from the Premier League in last place and the ill-fated reign of former Manchester United striker Ole Gunnar Solskjaer as manager, the club were in no position to make an immediate return to the top flight. The fury aimed at Tan showed no signs of relenting.

He was blamed by many during the club's stagnation under Russell Slade, who in one bizarre press conference in February 2016 appeared to confirm he was listening to the novice footballing advice from Tan for Cardiff's players to "shoot more, shoot from 30 yards".

Tan told BBC Wales: "In every match I want to see 30 or 40 attempts on goal." In the past there had been rumours he'd questioned why his goalkeepers were not scoring any goals.

"The players sat and listened to that, they saw the logic of taking opportunities when they come to them," added Slade. It was another illustration of just how rudderless the club had become.

By that stage, Tan had at least reversed the rebrand, prompting many Cardiff fans to flock back briefly to see their side play in blue, only to realise the football under Slade was drab and unambitious.

The key change was not just the appointment of Warnock, but the resignation of TG as chairman in March 2013 to be replaced by Mehmet Dalman, the former financier whose CV had included spells with Deutsche Bank and Credit Suisse.

It would prove to be a key moment in the Bluebirds' history, partly because Dalman's presence allowed Tan to take a backseat.

Dalman was said to have been influential in the appointment of Solskjaer, who he firmly believed would grow into a promising manager for the long-term. But the Norwegian was the wrong man at the wrong time in South Wales. His lavish spending policy burdened the club with debts and players who didn't fit in, nor could his squad salvage Premier League survival.

Dalman dutifully accepted the club had to part ways with Solskjaer in September 2014.

Both the chairman and owner would learn from their mistakes, however, and this was crystallised in the Warnock era. Joined by Ken Choo as chief executive and the shrewd executive director Steve Borley on the board, the quartet found their man in Warnock and Dalman in particular wasn't going to let that slip.

Gone were the days of Tan's shooting advice to strikers, or controversial decisions that disrupted the football side of the business. Warnock and Dalman were too experienced to let that happen.

"Vincent had his moments, but then he's the owner," says Warnock. "He'd often send me WhatsApp messages and try and tell me where I was going wrong. But he did it for the right reasons, he cared."

Warnock and Tan did indeed have their moments. There were disagreements, times when Warnock became upset and agitated after calls to Malaysia. He relied on the calming voice of wife Sharon to reassure him when times were tough and on one occasion she even wrote Tan an email detailing her husband's frustrations.

But the fact Tan stayed largely away from Cardiff City Stadium for matches and channeled the bulk of communication through Dalman – the buffer, in Warnock's words – allowed the club to operate smoothly. It became clear that, when it came to football, Warnock was in charge.

"It's only because he cares and because he doesn't

understand football that much," adds Warnock. "He understands the financial side but it was difficult to try to explain things. That's where Mehmet came in.

"But without Vincent's support we couldn't have done it. So I've got nothing bad to say about him really. I was pleased that I managed to get Cardiff promoted because he'd put so much money in and he could get some back.

"It was because of Mehmet, he was the buffer. He was articulate. Poor Ken Choo got the brunt of the stuff off Vincent a lot and he kept it off me as well. It was a team effort, really."

After arriving in Cardiff as manager, Warnock also introduced himself to the office staff, the cleaners and the tea ladies, as he put it. He took it upon himself to ensure those previously disparate factions felt part of the cause as much as Tan, Choo and Dalman did. "All singing from the same hymn sheet," was a phrase he used frequently in press conferences.

"They all needed help, they just needed bringing together, just like when I went to Sheffield United," says Warnock, who managed the team he supported as a boy, the Blades, between 1999 and 2007 – his longest stint as a manager.

"With the people in the offices it was all, 'They don't

talk to them and they don't talk to them' and the cliques. I think the crowd was 8,000 or something when I took over at Sheffield United and when I left after seven years, we'd got an average crowd of 25,000, a 30,000-seat stadium, an academy built... all the club was together.

"And that's how I wanted Cardiff. I thought they needed me more than I needed them. I thought I can't lose, so I'll go and give it my best shot.

"The fans wanted help, like Vincent wanted help."

* * * *

As Warnock's relationship with Dalman, and by proxy Tan, solidified, matters on the pitch began to take care of themselves and the fans were quickly on board. The Bristol City game had been a turning point for everyone, with the players suddenly motivated to build momentum and Warnock energised as he sought to emulate and then eclipse his Rotherham heroics with a bigger and more financially robust club.

Managing the supporters would be a more straightforward task in those early months for Warnock. He has always been more comfortable sharing a joke with fans while stepping off a team bus than negotiating with corporate men in the boardroom.

A 2-1 Severnside derby victory in his debut game as manager was always going to endear Warnock to fans. But the speed and manner in which the mood changed around the club was remarkable. Talk of relegation soon became ancient history as the Bluebirds quickly moved up the table, away from trouble.

"From the Bristol City game there was a definite change in how we regarded ourselves and how the fans thought of the club," says Cardiff supporter Aled Blake, author of *Bluebirds Reunited.*

"From that moment it was just a breath of fresh air and after such a long time when we'd felt the club was directionless, he gave a new impetus straight away and that just built and built with the turnaround in performances and the results in that first season."

Cardiff fans, who had longed to feel that sense of unity, who had craved to strive for a common purpose, suddenly had what they wanted. The football wasn't always free-flowing but the games were full of drama with a manager and a team who cared desperately about every single kick.

"I thought, 'Wow, watching Cardiff City is going to be exciting again', and it was," adds Aled Blake. "It didn't matter that we played long-ball football because the games would have something to talk about. It wasn't drab, the manager always had something to say."

There was no doubt Warnock had brought a thrill back to Cardiff City that fans hadn't felt since the Ninian Park days, the tenure of Dave Jones and his high-scoring, promotion-pushing team of the late noughties.

"It was what the club needed because the stadium was emptying, people had lost patience and were losing that passion you need as a football fan," says Blake. "And he was the guy who brought it all back. The Bristol City game set it all up."

The Bluebirds eked out 15 points from Warnock's first 10 games. It wasn't promotion form, but it was enough to steer them clear of the drop zone. Six wins from nine games in January and February – including milestone victories away at rivals Leeds (0-2), Derby (3-4) and Bristol City (2-3) – put Warnock's men in the top half of the Championship.

Mission accomplished then, though Warnock's next job was to temper the expectations of some supporters who were hungry for an immediate play-off push. It was a season too soon, the Cardiff manager insisted.

"We're looking to next season," he told reporters after

a 2-1 defeat to QPR in March. "I'm learning all the time – I saw one or two things today which really helped me decide what I'm going to do at the end of the season."

Cardiff finished the 2016/17 campaign in 12th, 18 points off the play-off positions and 11 points clear of relegation. Firmly mid-table.

In the penultimate match of the season – and the final home game – the Bluebirds were beaten 2-0 by promoted Newcastle who were crowned champions with that victory.

"We're going up, they're going down… going up, going down," went the lyrics of the Magpies fans' song that night, referencing rivals Sunderland's corresponding relegation from the Premier League.

Looking over at the delirious Newcastle fans at Cardiff City Stadium, Warnock gritted his teeth and told himself, 'Those celebrations will belong to us in 12 months' time'.

He was sure of it. Quite frankly, he'd spoken of very little else in the previous couple of months.

The dogwork had been done, the foundations laid. He'd managed up, he'd managed down.

CHAPTER FIVE

Seven Days Of Summer

It was on the patio of Neil Warnock's countryside home in a small Cornish village that Cardiff City's objectives for the 2017/18 season were set in stone.

Warnock had, of course, already been putting into motion his plans to win a record eighth career promotion. And while in the latter part of 2016/17 he had been pushed in interviews about his longer term aims with Bluebirds, he vocalised these very firm intentions to his players at a team barbecue in July 2017. It proved to be a fateful summer's night.

Promotion rivals Wolves went to Austria on their preseason tour that year. Aston Villa toured Germany, while Fulham took in both those countries plus Poland. Leeds

United went to Italy, Sheffield Wednesday to Portugal. In previous years Cardiff themselves had jetted to America and the Far East.

Warnock took his squad to Devon and Cornwall.

The location was chosen partly due to Warnock's affection for it. He has been based in Cornwall with his wife Sharon and youngest child William since falling in love with the area in the mid-1990s while managing Plymouth Argyle.

But the decision to take an aspirational Championship club on pre-season tour to the South West corner of England – and a county not known for its footballing heritage – was chiefly about building a sense of unity.

The barbecues, the fishing expeditions and golf trips – they were as important as the football, with Cardiff playing three first team games and the Under-23s playing twice.

Bar a drizzly night at Bodmin Town, when the Cardiff coach was too big to manoeuvre into the club car park and the players had to walk the remainder of the journey, the week had gone without a hitch, the other games played in pleasant July temperatures under sunny skies.

And having seen his side swat aside South West Peninsula League opponents AFC Tavistock and Bodmin and edge past his former side Plymouth at Home Park, Warnock gathered the players at his house for the most important part of the seven-day trip.

"They were all sat out the back of our house, all around with their drinks and burgers and what have you," explains Warnock.

"I always said a few words in pre-season and this time I said, 'Look lads, we've had a good week here, and this is the start of what's going to be one of the best seasons in your lives'."

The squad fell silent, the small talk disappeared in the warm summer air. All eyes were on one man.

"I said, 'We were going to have highs and lows, ups and downs, arguments, you're not going to like me at times, I'm going to leave some of you out, but if we stick as a team, I know we can get promotion'.

"I said, 'You've just got to trust me'."

Some players were more keen to believe than others, and Warnock knew he still had work to do, both on the training field and in the transfer market. Aron Gunnarsson went across to his manager later in the evening and wondered if the gin and tonics had already begun to take their toll during the speech.

The night went on, with Warnock instructing the club's

fitness gurus Carl Serrant and Lee Southernwood to relax their rules on nutrition for the evening. Warnock adds: "Carl wanted them to have chicken and rice and all that rubbish. But I said, 'No, not at my barbecue you're not, you're having bloody burgers and sausages'."

Yet despite the general feeling of merriment, Warnock's promotion battle cry stuck in the players' minds. Many would quickly forget the 7-2 win at Tavistock and the 3-1 triumph over Bodmin, but aspirations of promotion would stay with them all.

"There were two things about those tours," says Sol Bamba, who was quick to reinforce Warnock's message to any doubters in the squad at the time.

"First of all, the gaffer has got a good heart and he wanted to give back to the community. So playing against local teams gave them a good opportunity to play against a Championship or Premier League club and obviously for them to generate money as well.

"But also, and more importantly for me, was getting everyone together round his house. He introduced us to his wife and his kids.

"It created the atmosphere of a big family and people felt they could talk about anything. Because before being football players, we're all human beings and it was the feeling of 'if anyone needs anything, I'll be there for them, my wife will be there for them and even my kids will be there for them'."

It resonated with so many players. It was more evidence, to them, that Warnock was the master man-manager that they needed. Not just a footballing leader, but a personal mentor. The atmosphere was enough to persuade Sean Morrison to reject a lucrative wage offer from Sheffield Wednesday, who had tabled a £5million bid for the Cardiff captain. Morrison told Warnock he wanted to stay and a new contract was announced.

Bamba, Junior Hoilett and Lee Peltier also signed new deals that summer, as did Gunnarsson and Gabonese defender Bruno Ecuele Manga. Everyone wanted to be part of Warnock's special season, which was vital for stability within the camp.

"It was massive," continues Bamba. "I share the same values as him, as a family man. Before the glory and the football, we're all mums, dads, brothers and sisters.

"For the new lads coming into the squad, it was great. For them to go to the manager's house, have a drink, play some golf, do a bit of fishing, I'm sure they'd never done that with a manager before and I know that created a huge bond for the rest of the season: that we stick together."

Greg Halford was a more peripheral member of the squad than Bamba and Morrison, but he felt something stir inside, too. He'd won promotion before under various managers, but this was something different. Few managers can generate such team spirit with a humble trip to Cornwall.

"We trained pretty much on a cow field," reveals Halford, although the squad were accommodated at the more salubrious St Mellion golf resort.

"We had our down time playing golf and stuff like that and obviously went to Neil's house. It was brilliant.

"Pre-season is the most important part of the campaign to get the players together. Obviously to get fit too, but it's that bonding part. He's in his element when he's down in Cornwall and it brings the best from him and the players."

* * * *

Warnock would repeat the Cornwall trip the next pre-season, while preparing Cardiff for a campaign in the Premier League. Both years, too, he organised a charity match against local South Wales amateur side Taff's

Well. He turned up on a night in July 2017 to a small field on the outskirts of Cardiff with a squad packed full of Championship regulars. The first event of a vital pre-season.

It was a memorable night, when almost 3,000 Bluebirds fans crammed around the Rhiw'r Ddar recreation ground to watch the match. And it was much appreciated by the Taff's Well locals. Before the game, they had grabbed selfies and autographs from their favourite Cardiff City stars – including Warnock himself.

It was a blissful, sun-soaked evening, which preceded the Cornwall tour and where the atmosphere of total unity began to grow.

It also gave supporters the first glimpse of new signings: goalkeeper Neil Etheridge and winger Nathaniel Mendez-Laing, who had signed from Walsall and Rochdale respectively, as well as French midfielder Loic Damour, a complete unknown quantity, and former Rotherham striker Danny Ward. These were not marquee names who particularly excited fans, but they would become integral parts of the Warnock project.

"I remember when I was at QPR, I signed Shaun Derry and Clint Hill," says Warnock. "And the QPR fans said, 'Who the hell are these also-rans?'

"And it was similar here. 'Who the hell is Mendez-Laing? He got released from Wolves, he's been playing at Rochdale' and Etheridge from Walsall."

Warnock had been eyeing both players since the previous January window. And they weren't opportunistic bargains, despite both signing on free transfers; they were the result of some diligent background and scouting work, thanks to Warnock's wide web of football contacts.

Kevin Blackwell, a former goalkeeper himself, had identified Etheridge as an option between the posts, while Warnock was tipped off by one of his loyal former players, Christian Short – who'd played under him at Scarborough, Notts County and Huddersfield – about Mendez-Laing.

"We did our homework on those players," Warnock adds. "Even when we weren't working, Blacky [Blackwell] and Ronnie Jepson had been looking at certain players.

"Christian, one of my old players who's [a fitness coach] at Oxford now, rang me and said, 'I've seen a player for you, whenever you get a club, Mendez-Laing'. He said I'd love him."

It was rarely straightforward for Warnock in the transfer market at Cardiff, however, and even some elements of these understated deals proved tricky.

Mendez-Laing and his agent were en route to Wigan Athletic when the call came from Warnock. Following a very literal U-turn and the promise of a better salary, he eventually became a Cardiff player.

Cardiff and Walsall had argued over Etheridge's valuation in January, but with the goalkeeper out of contract in the summer, it became an easier transaction.

The fifth arrival of the summer was also not without a snag. Warnock identified Hearts defender Callum Paterson as the solution to his dilemma at right-back, but had to persuade Vincent Tan to part with £400,000 to compensate the Scottish club, who were losing the 22-year-old at the end of his contract.

Paterson was also badly injured with an ACL issue and wasn't due back until December. The Cardiff transfer committee, comprising Warnock, Mehmet Dalman, Ken Choo and Steve Borley, were satisfied that he was worth the risk.

But Warnock wanted one more thing before he could be satisfied with his squad: flair.

It had previously been provided by creative linchpin Peter Whittingham (who tragically passed away a matter of months before this book was published). And although Warnock was happy to offer the Bluebirds favourite a one-year contract extension, he rebuked the player's demand for an extra two years. Whittingham was hugely talented but, approaching his 33rd birthday, was down on energy and pace. In Warnock's mind he was replaceable and so Whittingham bid farewell to the club, with a heavy heart, after a decade of service and joined Blackburn.

Former England international Rickie Lambert and Craig Noone were among the others deemed surplus to requirements.

"I felt sorry for one or two of them because they were coming to the end of their careers and they just couldn't do what I wanted them to," Warnock recalls. "It wasn't their fault and it wasn't their fault they'd been given good contracts."

And so in search of that much-needed creativity, Cardiff turned to a familiar foe: Lee Tomlin.

The Bristol City playmaker had been a thorn in Warnock's side during that opening game in charge, Tomlin scoring the Robins' goal that kept the game on a knife-edge. Watching the stocky yet silky number 10 evoked memories of a previous Warnock favourite, QPR hero Adel Taarabt.

Warnock ranks the Moroccan among his greatest ever achievements in one-to-one man-management. He remains arguably the only boss to have got the best from Taarabt, a former Tottenham player whose career since working with Warnock at QPR has been nomadic.

"It would be easy to toss him to one side, but I have a lot of time for him and he is a lovely lad," Warnock once said about the frustration of working with Taarabt, immensely talented but equally infuriating. A true maverick.

Tomlin was the same. He wasn't going to stick to Warnock's disciplined defensive blueprint, but such was the need for a creative spark, Cardiff forked out £1.5million for the new wearer of Whittingham's old number seven shirt.

"Tomlin was the marquee signing – but that was emblematic of Warnock's transfer record really," says Aled Blake. "He was so good at bringing in players on the cheap, for little money, that when he did spend they'd seem to be destined to fail. So the summer signings, with the exception of Tomlin, I don't think fans felt they were going to set the world alight."

It was therefore ironic that Etheridge, Mendez-Laing and Paterson – and arguably even Ward and Damour – would go on to have greater impacts than Tomlin over the course of the season that followed.

Tomlin was a bystander for much of pre-season, too,

with Warnock citing fitness issues as the reason for his delayed involvement. Yet when he set up Kenneth Zohore for the only goal in the 1-0 win at Plymouth to round off the tour, hopes were high – not just for Tomlin, for the whole squad and the season ahead.

And while you would have struggled to find a Cardiff fan feeling pessimistic about the imminent campaign, it would have been an exaggeration to say many harboured realistic hopes of promotion. The bookmakers certainly didn't rate the Bluebirds' chances. It seemed a push for the play-offs would be their best bet.

"We were mid-table with the bookies," says Warnock. "We weren't even in the top eight with the odds. We were about 12th.

"And that's when, when the lads went off for a walk or a swim or whatever after the barbecue, Gunnarsson said to me, 'What was in your glass when you said that? Did you mean that or did you just say it?'

"I said, 'Gunnars, of course I did'. I had seven promotions; left, right and centre and I'd never felt like that for a long time. I had the best chairman I'd had for many years and the club was geared to success. We had unbelievable fans and we knew we could give them something they'd not had for a while."

On paper, Cardiff ended the summer of 2017 with eight rather underwhelming signings – including deadline day loan arrivals Craig Bryson and Liam Feeney and striker Omar Bogle – plus the enigmatic Tomlin. They had beaten two amateur sides, as well as Plymouth and Scottish team Livingston, and lost to Shrewsbury. Warnock had spent less than £4million in transfer fees.

A section of supporters doubted the transfer policy and while the bookmakers completely dismissed Cardiff's promotion chances, this only served to heighten the togetherness inside the camp.

Warnock was king of the siege mentality. The low-key signings and the low-key pre-season tour allowed Cardiff to fly under the radar – with no big egos in their squad – ready to upset the odds.

"I think it was just the personalities more than anything else," explains Halford. "Neil has been able to master that over his career and get those personalities to fit into what he wants. We were very close-knit: we'd go out for meals together on a regular basis, we'd do outside activities with each other after training.

"There were no cliques in the group – this was literally a whole 24-man team. We did everything together and the lads that got promoted still talk to each other now."

So they were ready. The ultimate underdogs? With the new season approaching, the bookies, the Championship experts and big-hitters like Wolves, Aston Villa, Fulham and Leeds were about to find out just how much they had underestimated Cardiff City.

CHAPTER SIX

The Surge

Wolves 1-2 Cardiff, 19th August 2017
Wolves (3-4-3): Ruddy; Miranda, Coady, Boly;
Doherty, Saiss (Ronan, 83), Neves, Douglas (Dicko, 78);
Enobakhare (Cavaleiro, 58), Jota, Bonatini.
Subs not used: Norris, Batth, Bennett, Price.
Cardiff (4-3-3): Etheridge; Peltier, Morrison, Bamba;
Richards; Gunnarsson, Damour (Manga, 90), Ralls;
Mendez-Laing, Hoilett (Ward, 83), Zohore.
Subs not used: Murphy, Halford, Tomlin, Kennedy, Bogle.
Wolves goal: Bonatini (67).
Cardiff goals: Ralls (54), Mendez-Laing (77).

Form is such a fragile thing in football. As Neil Warnock once said himself, teams lose momentum much more quickly than they can build it. Events can conspire against you, outcomes can change in an instance. One defeat can bring the entire house of cards to the ground.

But when Kenneth Zohore curled sensationally into the top corner in the 88th minute of Cardiff City's season opener against Burton Albion – sending the travelling Bluebirds packed into one end of the diminutive Pirelli Stadium into raptures – you could sense it was a momentum-shifting moment.

All that pre-season positivity, the togetherness and the belief came coursing back through the veins of players, fans and manager alike.

Cardiff had laboured against Burton, but continued to plug away and eventually got their reward. A week later, they thrashed promotion favourites Aston Villa 3-0 at home, then saw off Sheffield United 2-0 in midweek.

After three games, Warnock's men were top of the Championship with a 100 per cent record. They then travelled to Wolves – who boasted an identically perfect record – for an early season promotion ding-dong.

This was the real test for the harmony Warnock had grown in his Cardiff squad, not to mention their footballing prowess.

"The tour was huge in that start," says Sol Bamba, who had missed the end of the previous campaign with injury but was now enjoying his best spell of form for years. He revealed there were plenty of financial incentives too, in order to ensure the Bluebirds squad were on their mettle from the first kick.

"In any promotion he'd had before, he said the start was massive," adds Bamba on Warnock.

"He wanted us to start well. And looking at it from the business-side, he spoke to the owner and made sure for the first 10 games, the players had big win bonuses, so everyone was happy."

New boys Neil Etheridge and Nathaniel Mendez-Laing were particularly happy, having forced their way into the first-choice side, which Warnock only made slight adjustments to during the first five matches. The likes of Omar Bogle, Danny Ward and Lee Tomlin had arrived as new forward options, but couldn't get a run of games.

Mendez-Laing – who came off the bench at Burton – scored twice against Villa, embarrassing former England captain John Terry for one goal. He also scored in the Sheffield United win and against Portsmouth in a 2-1 League Cup victory.

"Mendez was unbelievable that day," Greg Halford says, remembering the Villa game.

"When he was focussed solely on football, there weren't

many players who could defend against him in that league. It's just that focus that you need to get into him. He has the ability to do whatever he wants and that day against Aston Villa, he showed what he can do."

Cardiff were on fire. Yet the league season was only three games old and the critics remained unconvinced, as first met second on a warm August afternoon at Molineux.

Wolves were the overwhelming favourites – not just to win this contest, but for automatic promotion – having invested heavily in their squad in the summer. With the financial help of Chinese ownership consortium Fosun and noted 'super agent' Jorge Mendes, who represented Cristiano Ronaldo among others, they made a series of ambitious changes.

They replaced Paul Lambert with former Valencia and Porto manager Nuno Espirito Santo. He, along with Portuguese Under-21 stars Ruben Neves and Diogo Jota, were extraordinarily bold recruitments for a Championship side.

It served as a statement of intent that sent shockwaves throughout the league. Wolves were serious this year. Neves and Jota both started the Cardiff game.

"They had everyone, didn't they?" Warnock laughs, remembering his preparations for that seismic clash.

It was like getting ready for that Bristol City game all over again. The Cardiff players had fire in their bellies, this time with the confidence of a side that had won four from four in all competitions before the trip to Wolverhampton.

Having faced Sheffield United in midweek there may have been fears about fatigue, but Warnock was never afraid of allowing his players to rest. They had all the motivation and preparation they needed.

"That week they were so het up," Warnock says. "I said to them, 'We can win this game and we can make a few people sit up and take notice, because we're good enough'. When I looked at their individuals and ours I thought we'd got a great chance."

The atmosphere was febrile, just the way Warnock liked it. Even walking through the town to the gold-trimmed Molineux Stadium, it felt as though a huge event was taking place. The importance of the game was lost on nobody, not least Warnock and Nuno, who would begin a fierce rivalry that afternoon.

The game's early knockings saw Cardiff, full of energy and endeavour, hunt down the Wolves players in packs. Hounded for the ball, hustled into mistakes, the hosts looked rattled.

It appeared, in this opening spell of the season, that Warnock and his staff had brought a new dimension to Cardiff's football. On that day against Wolves this was encapsulated by Mendez-Laing, who gave wing-back Barry Douglas a torrid time all afternoon.

Cardiff were solid at the back, industrious in midfield and razor-sharp in attack. Their early dominance very nearly brought a goal for Bamba, but his header cannoned off the crossbar.

Wolves had plenty of nous to go with their precocious Portuguese talents and they soon steadied the ship, almost levelling through Jota on 33 minutes.

It remained goalless at half-time, though a robust challenge from Loic Damour – picked ahead of Tomlin to bolster the midfield – on Romain Saiss prompted a furious backlash from the Molineux crowd and the Wolves coaching staff. They believed Damour should have seen red for an alleged elbow. Referee Scott Duncan brandished a yellow.

"Every decision that we got on the sideline, Nuno and about 10 of his staff were standing up, appealing every time," says Warnock.

"It was really hostile, it was brilliant. I've always enjoyed going to Molineux, the fans are good and it's a good atmosphere. And we played some good stuff. We defended well but then we broke well."

Warnock was given a barrage of abusive chants from the Wolves fans throughout the game, but took it all in good spirit. He had the backing of a vocal Cardiff away following in any case and was focussed on the pulsating contest.

Cardiff kept fighting and got their deserved break 10 minutes into the second half when Joe Ralls turned the ball into the bottom corner, after an Aron Gunnarsson tackle caught Wolves cold and Junior Hoilett raced forward, feeding the onrushing Ralls.

The lead didn't last long. Wolves had thrown on key winger Ivan Cavaleiro, whose shot was parried by Etheridge and ended up at the feet of Douglas. His cross was prodded in by Leo Bonatini to make it 1-1 and suddenly Cardiff were under the cosh.

They weathered the Wolves storm and inevitably Mendez-Laing won it, after good work from Zohore opened up space for the irrepressible right-winger to thump the ball home. A couple of vital Etheridge saves maintained the 2-1 scoreline.

"We just played such good football and it was a thoroughly deserved win," Warnock says.

"Even a couple of mates of mine who are Wolves fans said we deserved it. The fans were amazing across the opposite side of the pitch, it was just a great afternoon. It surprised everybody, nobody thought we could do that. But it didn't surprise me or the lads."

Warnock's side had won a rip-roaring top of the table contest against arguably the best team in the division. And they completely merited the three points.

Mendez-Laing, who had come through the Wolves academy as a youngster before dropping down the divisions, now had five goals in four Cardiff starts.

"The penny has finally dropped with him," former Wolves striker Chris Iwelumo told Channel 5's highlights show that night, on Mendez-Laing.

"He was a young boy at Wolves when I was there and you could see the quality but it just wasn't consistent. And he's done what a lot of players do, they go down the levels and it sinks in. [Cardiff] know the qualities they've got and he's delivering."

He was a revelation and a crucial part of this new all-action Cardiff City team, which fans were adoring.

Even more significant, perhaps, was Nuno's reaction after the game. He conceded that his Wolves side were cowed, outfought and unable to deal with the visitors' physicality. "Cardiff's game plan was to be aggressive," he said. "We have to be mentally strong to deal with this kind of provocation. We made too many mistakes for a team that wants to be strong."

In the end, Nuno's players learned a valuable lesson from that August afternoon: how to handle sides like Cardiff, and this added resilience brought them promotion as champions at the end of the season.

For that reason and the impact on Cardiff's own fortunes, those 90 minutes were arguably the most significant of the entire Championship 2017/18 campaign. These two teams had set the standard for the rest of the league and it was clear, with their own inimitable styles, they would dominate the headlines.

The following week, Cardiff beat QPR 2-1 at home, securing a fifth consecutive win; the best ever start to a campaign in the club's history.

* * * *

How were they able to start so well?

On the surface the reasons appeared clear: a unique collective spirit, a footballing style that was effective at both ends and a charismatic manager binding it all together. But within the squad there was more to it. No doubt the pre-season tour had played a huge role in building momentum.

Also, Kevin Blackwell's man-marking system in defence had been outsmarting teams from a tactical perspective, while extra pace gave them more cutting edge on the counter-attack.

Many argue that Warnock's Cardiff never played better football than that five-game spell in August 2017.

"That was our best time, it gave us the platform to go and win promotion," insists Bamba.

"During the Christmas time we lost four on the bounce, but because of that start we had enough of a points cushion to stay towards the top. We never went lower than third or fourth.

"And the attacking football we were playing was unbelievable. Mendez-Laing was on fire, the shape was good, we were solid at the back. That was definitely our best time."

Promotion was no longer a mere pipe dream. And those hopes of going up could no longer be contained within the camp. The Cardiff supporters sensed something special was happening.

"It set our expectations up even further," says Aled Blake. "Beginning the season in the way we did and after the pre-season stuff he did – which was really different and worthwhile – it was all about engineering a togetherness at the club again. That was within the squad and with the fans as well."

Blackwell, too, cited the humility of a close-knit squad, and the confidence instilled in creative sparks like Hoilett and Mendez-Laing, as a key reason for their early success.

"We went under the radar because we didn't go spouting that confidence off outside the group. You don't want to end up with egg on your face," he said.

"But quietly we told the players they had a good chance if they worked hard and stuck to what we believed in. We were always positive with them. We told the wingers that they were fantastic at going past people and to be aggressive."

The timing of the purple patch, 10 months into Warnock's reign, suggests the club had now settled into a rhythm of structure under his leadership. Players had become accustomed to his methods and the likes of Sean Morrison, Aron Gunnarsson and Joe Ralls – who had been at Cardiff throughout the years of discord – finally felt settled.

This environment also allowed new players to flourish. Warnock has proven popular with players at a number of clubs, not just because he's such an affable person with a good sense of humour.

He has admitted to being much more of a motivator than a tactician and at Cardiff he settled into a pattern, which allowed assistant boss Blackwell and first-team coach Ronnie Jepson to take the majority of training sessions. Warnock handled the man-management and gave the players complete clarity.

"When I work with Neil, it leaves myself and Ronnie free to concentrate on the training ground and the opposition," added Blackwell.

"As a manager, you've got to be able to trust people around you to give you the right information. I've done over 500 games as a manager and I always wanted someone around me who could give honest feedback when the heat was on.

"Ronnie and I try to take as much pressure off Neil's shoulders when we can and provide cold, calculated answers. We try to clear the fog."

Warnock's habit of giving players extra days off, allowing them to rest rather than spend needless hours in the gym – which he felt could cause fatigue-related injuries – also went down well with the squad. There was a very distinct formula and during those early weeks of the season it was working like a dream.

"Management is not just about picking a side and doing your coaching," explains Warnock.

"A lot of it is telling the lads what they should and shouldn't do. A lot of the young lads when they're doing well, they just want to do more training. And you've got to be so careful with athletes."

Warnock received no complaints, even from the likes of Hoilett and Mendez-Laing, who were in flying form that August and wanted to train as much as possible. The manager used his experience to channel his players' aggression in the correct way, while Blackwell's training ground work allowed Cardiff to "tactically nullify the opposition", as he put it.

The men would themselves admit this never worked better than in the opening weeks of 2017/18 campaign. The victory over Wolves, the winning streak and the swell of good feeling around the place had put the club on cloud nine.

But they still had plenty of convincing to do for those on the outside. There was a long season ahead in the Championship, 41 games to be precise, and it would be an almighty struggle at times. Neil Warnock and Cardiff City needed to prove that they truly were promotion contenders.

CHAPTER SEVEN

The Warnock Way

What is it that defines a great football team?

Admirers of Manchester City's greatest ever manager, Pep Guardiola, would argue that it's style, playing with a stated ethos that produces attractive, attacking football. Fans of his managerial rival Jose Mourinho would say the opposite: that football is a results business and being effective trumps everything else.

Style or substance? Both men have won Premier League and Champions League titles in the modern era.

This dualism was put into stark contrast when the two managers were in charge of Spain's two behemoth clubs: Barcelona and Real Madrid respectively. El Clasico matches were no longer just a rivalry of teams, but a battle of footballing philosophies, with the opposing styles in many ways reflective of the historical and social differences between the two Spanish cities.

Mourinho was depicted as the vandal trying to spoil Guardiola's art. The Catalan won the hearts of the public across Europe while Mourinho was sacked, deemed unsuitable to manage a club of Madrid's stature.

As Neil Warnock will tell you, there is no right or wrong way to play the game.

Yet the debate on footballing styles was one that dominated discussions around Cardiff City throughout the 2017/18 campaign, particularly during their promotion battle with Fulham.

Slavisa Jokanovic's side were the first team to stop Cardiff from winning that season, dominating a September meeting at Craven Cottage that the Bluebirds snatched a point from, thanks to Danny Ward's late equaliser. The manner in which Fulham had played during that 1-1 draw was quite something. They had a free-flowing brand of attacking football centred around stand-out individuals like Tom Cairney, Ryan Sessegnon and Stefan Johansen. 'There's no doubt it was brilliant to watch.

Although Fulham remained mid-table for much of the campaign, their second meeting with the Bluebirds – a romping 4-2 win for the West London club at Cardiff

City Stadium – would precipitate a stunning streak of form. Fulham were outstanding in that Boxing Day clash and they soon proved they could outplay anyone in the division on their day.

Jokanovic's men shot up the table, enjoying a 23-game unbeaten run that lasted from mid-December until the final game of the season.

As the season wore on, it became clear Wolves would top the table, leaving Cardiff and Fulham to scrap it out for the second automatic promotion spot.

But it was during a Sky Sports debate between former Fulham and England midfielder Danny Murphy and ex-Bluebirds striker Craig Bellamy (who was also working as the club's academy chief at the time), that the issue of footballing styles came to a head in the media.

"You couldn't come across two more opposite teams in terms of how they play football," observed Bellamy. "But they're both having huge success from it."

He then hit upon a point that felt very relevant to Warnock and the criticism his team had received all season.

"There's become a snobbery in football," added Bellamy.

"I keep hearing the words 'right way of playing' – but there is no right and wrong way of playing. You just have to get results and Cardiff knew what they were doing when they brought Neil Warnock in.

"And it's not rocket science, it's route one and whether people like it or not – and opposition fans might want to boo it – they would much rather sit on our points... we're one win away from being in the Premier League."

Murphy reluctantly concurred, though reaffirmed his belief in a spiky debate that Fulham would be promoted automatically. On one occasion Bellamy snapped at him: "Stop saying 'right way', there's no right or wrong way to play!"

As an insider in the Cardiff camp, Bellamy was speaking with genuine insight into Warnock's methods, which he'd seen put into practice on the training ground. He accepted that the Bluebirds boss, from a tactical perspective, came from the Mourinho school of management, rather than Guardiola's.

Fellow pundit and former Cardiff folk hero Nathan Blake agrees that Warnock's football was unashamedly route one.

"The football was straightforward, but they did it well," he says. "They had a togetherness, like a family – 'us against the world' – that dictated everything. The fans had a manager who talked their kind of lingo."

Midway through the campaign, the supporters' vocabulary had a new term coined with regards to Cardiff's approach to winning games: the Warnock Way.

It meant to win ugly, to play football that was effective before anything else. Because after that opening surge of victories, played in a swashbuckling style, Cardiff found they often had to revert to a simpler method. They couldn't always find top gear.

Defeats away at Preston North End (3-0) and Birmingham City (1-0) in September and October had seen Cardiff's defence exposed and Warnock found his side lacking in creativity. He didn't risk his maverick playmaker Lee Tomlin as he couldn't track back in the way Warnock wanted. It had to be 4-5-1 with players like Joe Ralls, Craig Bryson or Loic Damour bursting forward from midfield to join sole striker Kenneth Zohore.

Full-backs Lee Peltier and Joe Bennett would rarely contribute to the attack. Often Warnock played a centre-back, in Bruno Manga, on the right side of his back four. Occasionally it would even be a five-man defensive line.

Cardiff's game plan was to keep things tight at the back and play no-risk football: no dicey passes in deep positions, long balls when necessary, man-marking every attacking runner.

Bamba adds: "The gaffer would say, 'I know you can play', but he didn't want us to take any risks in our box or near our goals, because it can be a goal straight away.

"I don't think there's anything wrong with that. We'd start to play good football in the final third. We wouldn't take any risks in our own half, but from the halfway line we'd start playing football."

For the most part, it worked and brought about another spell of solid form – just one defeat in 10 games in November and December. But the football also prompted new waves of criticism from the media and opposition managers.

Just as Nuno Espirito Santo had accused Cardiff of physical provocation in September, Nottingham Forest manager Mark Warburton took a swipe at perceived time-wasting by Warnock's players after a 2-0 Bluebirds win at the City Ground on 26th November.

"We were frustrated at many things," said Warburton. "The continual delaying. We have to learn, Cardiff are very good at what they do."

"They're organised, strong and powerful and when they got two goals up you know they're going to slow the game down," said an exasperated Brentford boss Dean Smith after a 2-0 win for Cardiff in the same period.

The intimations were clear. Cardiff weren't playing fairly, in the minds of these opposition managers. Bitterness? Or did they have a point?

Many of the comments were unfair. But as Sol Bamba reveals, the Cardiff players didn't care either way.

"Me personally? It didn't affect me at all," he says. "What mattered was the result at the end. I'm a very pragmatic player so I always thought whatever you needed to do to win the game, you did it. That's where the gaffer said I was important for the team.

"Don't get me wrong, there were conversations between the players in training sometimes and we said we'd love to play the way Pep Guardiola plays with City, for example. But I always said, 'Who cares?' What mattered was winning games and it didn't matter if we won promotion winning ugly."

Warnock had retained Sean Morrison as his captain when he first arrived at the club, for stability reasons. But he knew Bamba was his chief lieutenant in the dressing room, so ensured the centre-back quashed any lingering frustrations from players who harboured aspirations of playing another, more expansive, way. As both men knew, it simply wouldn't have worked for Cardiff.

"I know in the team, some players wanted to play a

different way. But we tried that before and it didn't take us anywhere," explains Bamba.

"The medical staff used to say, 'We're back to the Warnock Way'. Every now and then we'd try to play out from the back – and we would get found out. So we did whatever worked for our team.

"That's why the gaffer is so good, he adapted to the players he had in his squad.

"Sometimes the criticism he got – and it's not just because I love the man and I'll defend him whatever – but it was criticism for the wrong reasons."

* * * *

Now if there's one football manager who can handle his fair share of flak, it's Warnock. He's well aware of his reputation as a Marmite Man – love him or hate him – and has been known to play up to that stereotype, revelling in winding up opposition managers, players or supporters.

The 2005 fly-on-the-wall documentary entitled simply *Warnock*, charting a season at Sheffield United under his management, gives a no-holds-barred view of the South Yorkshireman and shows he is unafraid of confrontation. But the criticism did sting at times in 2017/18, as he felt his Cardiff side – who never dropped out of the Championship top four all season – weren't getting the plaudits their results deserved.

Goals like Ward's stunner at Nottingham Forest, or the stunning team goal capped by Kenneth Zohore against Leeds – or a raft of Junior Hoilett screamers – weren't being spoken about.

Even from experienced pundits like Danny Murphy, the compliments were back-handed. Warnock would regularly claim in press conferences that his team were underrated, unheralded.

"Obviously I'm always criticised about a certain way of playing," he says. "Even now when they refer to the current [Cardiff] side, they always talk about Warnock's team and how Warnock was, 'the Warnock Way'.

"But there's no right or wrong way in football, you've just got to get the best out of the players you've got and decide how you're going to play."

Greg Halford was one of the players, along with Bamba and others, who was just delighted to be part of a winning side. He actually goes further than the Ivorian, suggesting the criticism drove the Bluebirds onto better things that season, further enhancing the siege mentality that existed within the squad.

"Yeah, we relished it to be honest," he smiles.

"It was like, 'Yeah, you play your way and lose, we'll play our way and win'. It didn't affect us. If we were putting results together and ahead of other teams in the league, they had no argument at all.

"Neil has his ways and it's served him unbelievably well throughout his career. And we all bought into his ways. Sometimes it wasn't the prettiest but it's not about being pretty – it's about winning games.

"This is what confuses me with some fans, who want to be entertained with good football, but if you end up losing on a Saturday you think, 'Surely it's just about winning?'"

Players privately admitted there were days when they stepped off the training field following a Kevin Blackwell and Ronnie Jepson session and wondered if the tactics they were drilling would be sophisticated enough to get the win that weekend. More often than not, they were.

It seemed primitive at times, And by Blackwell's own admission the instructions were basic, but tailored around stopping the other team from playing their game.

"What we tried to do in training was replicate what

would happen on a Saturday," explains Blackwell. "We worked on how to keep our shape when we were under pressure, also what we call 'handcuffs' at set plays – making sure people mark their opposite number tightly – and just reiterating basics.

"Sometimes it becomes normal for players to go to work and forget those basics. What people have also failed to notice is that tactically we nullified our opposition. Time and time again. You can talk about philosophies in football but you can't come into a club with a philosophy that doesn't suit the players. If the players can't play that way, you're knackered."

It just so happened that Fulham had the players to play Jokanovic's way. So Warnock and Cardiff played their own way too.

The stats told their own intriguing tale: Cardiff completed an average of 166 passes per 90 minutes – Guardiola's Man City won the Premier League with an average of 666 per game that year – and over the campaign Fulham and Wolves had the two best passing success rates. Meanwhile, Cardiff's rate of 59 per cent was the lowest in the Championship. And yet they won promotion alongside Fulham and Wolves, edging out Jokanovic's men in the fierce race for second place.

There is no doubt Cardiff's football became more attritional, and yet more effective, as the season progressed. By the time spring rolled around, another hot streak of eight successive wins had put Warnock's men on the brink of promotion.

They were bullying teams with their physicality, the perfect example being the 3-1 win at Brentford in March when, after a disastrous opening five minutes that saw them trail 1-0, Cardiff dug deep and turned the game on its head. Brentford's short passing style was overwhelmed by Warnock's direct approach.

The pace of Nathaniel Mendez-Laing and Hoilett on the wings remained crucial, as did Cardiff's height from set-pieces, yet a key tactical change during this period was to play Callum Paterson in the number 10 role.

The Scot had been signed as a right-back, but according to Warnock he "couldn't defend" so was accommodated higher up the pitch. Paterson was big and strong and worked his socks off for the team. He ended the season with 10 goals, the Bluebirds' highest league scorer. His opportunistic strike in that game at Brentford delighted Warnock.

The Paterson tactical masterstroke and the January signing of Bolton target man Gary Madine were representative of the direction in which the football was headed. Sometimes, it became the Warnock Way 'on steroids', as Nathan Blake said at the time. But with promotion edging closer by April, the veteran manager simply didn't care. It was about getting over the line.

As Bellamy said: "People say you can't play like that in the Premier League, but we'll deal with that later."

Of course Warnock would reassess everything at the end of the season. There was no doubt the Premier League would require something more refined. But beating Fulham to second place in the Championship was all that mattered in that moment.

"We had debates in the dressing room about the way Fulham played," reveals Bamba. "Nobody expected us to go up first of all, but even at the end people expected Fulham to catch up.

"Apparently they were playing 'the right way' and fair enough they played pretty football, but we finished second ahead of them and they had to go through the play-offs. Winning has always mattered most to me. It's not the way you win."

Cardiff did, of course, win the race. Both they and Fulham stuttered in the final furlong, the Bluebirds losing away to play-off sides Aston Villa and Derby, before a vital win at Hull City – secured by heroics from captain Sean Morrison – set up a thrilling final day showdown.

Footballing styles would count for very little during the season's finale as Fulham crumbled away at Birmingham, losing for the first time since 16th December. Cardiff held their nerve at home to Reading. Cue joyous celebrations.

The table said Cardiff were promoted in second place. Fulham, in third, would go into the play-offs. It didn't say anything about style.

CHAPTER EIGHT

Winter Of Discontent

The year 2017 had been a memorable one for Welsh football.

In June, the Champions League final was staged in Wales for the first time, with thousands of supporters from Real Madrid and Juventus cramming into Cardiff and the two teams contesting a memorable showpiece in which Cristiano Ronaldo – the world's best footballer – starred in a 4-1 win for Los Blancos. Hometown boy and Welsh favourite Gareth Bale celebrated with the national flag draped around him, an iconic image.

A month earlier, Cardiff City's South Wales rivals Swansea City had secured Premier League survival in dramatic fashion under manager Paul Clement, having recovered from a chaotic season that had seen three changes of manager. All the while Cardiff themselves were making steady if not headline-making progress under Neil Warnock, having laid the foundations for their promotion push during a quiet summer in Devon and Cornwall, before taking centre stage in August.

The early season winning run had created a buoyant mood around the club, which couldn't be punctured even by the odd poor result.

When Warnock's men did lose, or draw, it was usually dramatic. A November reverse at Bristol City's Ashton Gate was marked by Omar Bogle's controversial sending off; a 2-2 draw against Reading was clinched with a stoppage time Lee Tomlin equaliser, with the Bluebirds fighting back from 2-0 down. There were drab goalless draws at home to Derby and Millwall, but nothing too disastrous.

No, it would take four defeats within the space of 10 days at the end of the year to truly concern supporters and leave Warnock grappling for answers. Even the best teams go through blips of form, but this was unprecedented in Warnock's short Cardiff reign. Whenever they'd lost before, they'd always bounced back.

Sir Alex Ferguson once said the only virus that infected his Manchester United sides was 'winning' but Cardiff had caught something more serious; they had a winter bug known as 'losing'.

It was Christmas 2017, but nobody around Cardiff City Stadium was in a particularly festive mood.

Again, many of the questions centred around tactics. Because while a 2-0 defeat at Bolton Wanderers on 23rd December had seen Cardiff on the wrong end of a questionable penalty call – Sol Bamba penalised for a dubious handball – subsequent defeats to Fulham and Preston after Christmas Day saw them completely outplayed.

Had opponents finally sussed out Kevin Blackwell's tactical blueprint? Did this call for some more sophisticated instructions and a major rethink? Not according to Bamba.

"We never questioned the tactics," he insists.

"Obviously when you lose games everyone has to look at themselves, think about what they could have done better. People always said we play long ball, but what we did was work teams out. We watched the videos and worked out the strengths and weaknesses of the teams we were going to play against."

The methods barely changed, except Cardiff weren't 'working teams out' anymore and the momentum had dissipated. The team appeared to have lost confidence, despite the fact their league position never dropped lower than fourth.

The 1-0 home defeat to Preston on 29th December seemed to be the nadir. It was a strangely subdued affair in which Cardiff created next to nothing. There was no pace on the counter-attack, no penetration up front. Nathaniel Mendez-Laing hadn't scored since August. Kenneth Zohore was in and out of the side amid issues with fitness and form. Tom Clarke's scruffy 90th minute winner for Preston sent supporters home feeling deflated.

But Warnock, who had presided over his 1,400th game as a manager during this period, remained calm. This was his biggest test so far at Cardiff and thankfully for him, he retained the wholehearted support of the dressing room.

"We were never really worried," says Greg Halford. "Obviously we had meetings after games where we'd all chat in the dressing room and get to the bottom of it as quickly as possible.

"But there isn't a team in the Championship that doesn't go on a little bit of a bad spell. Four games is a very good bad spell, if you know what I mean. It was literally going back to basics, outworking teams and being more focussed. Doing what we were good at."

So the solution on the training ground was not to start over-complicating matters, but to strip things down even further. Also playing their part were an extraordinary number of injuries. As well as Zohore, Lee Peltier (hip), Kadeem Harris (ankle), Jazz Richards (ankle), Danny Ward (knee) and Craig Bryson (Achilles) had all been out for some time, leaving Bogle as the only fit striker.

But it was the absences of two key players, and close Warnock allies, Aron Gunnarsson and Sean Morrison, that were really taking their toll.

Gunnarsson had been a concern for Warnock for some time. He'd enjoyed a summer to savour with national team Iceland in 2016, knocking England out of Euro 2016, and as national team captain he felt a special sense of loyalty to his country. He even has a tattoo of the national flag emblazoned on his back. But he also risked burn-out every time he went on international duty, something Warnock had aired public grievances about. Injuries were a common issue.

In November, when Gunnarsson tried to return too soon from a lay-off, playing 21 minutes as a substitute against Brentford and then 74 minutes from the start three days later at Barnsley, he suffered a relapse. He would need ankle surgery and wouldn't play for Cardiff again until April. Although Warnock had signed Bryson and Loic Damour in the summer as midfield cover, it was a disaster to lose his midfield kingpin. Gunnarsson's early season form had been excellent.

Similarly, losing Morrison with a knee problem was a body blow – though many fans had hoped the partnership between Bamba and Bruno Manga would do the job in the captain's absence. Plenty had called for Manga to play ahead of Morrison when everyone was fit, though it soon became apparent that the skipper was a key cog, not just as a footballer and a defender, but as a leader.

Bamba was comfortable enough taking the armband but it was no coincidence that in Morrison's absence, Cardiff played five and lost four.

"Mozza had his critics because he's not a real fine player to look at, not a silky player," reflects Warnock. "And he had bad spells but I always stuck with him as he was my captain."

The final game without Morrison would test the manager in different ways. It could have been the moment the promotion push began to fall apart, with the gap to league leaders Wolves widening, while Derby and Bristol City were both in good form and making a play for second spot.

For the trip to QPR on 1st January, 2018, Warnock sprung a number of selection surprises and an apparent change in tactics.

New year, new me? It looked something like that, as goalkeeper Neil Etheridge was dropped for back-up Brian Murphy and lesser-spotted centre-back Matthew Connolly came into the defence for his first league appearance of the season. Youngster Rhys Healey was another surprise inclusion further up the pitch while a fit-again Peltier played out of position in central midfield.

The system was difficult to decipher, though from the early stages it appeared to be a 3-4-3 formation, never before seen from Warnock's Cardiff. It was haphazard and very unlike him. He had previously been reluctant to change his tactical template.

There's no doubt the selections were partly borne out of Cardiff's long injury list, but also out of Warnock's frustrations with his team's lapse. The changes didn't work, as the Bluebirds were beaten 2-1 at Loftus Road, with the manager furious at "Sunday League defending" for QPR's first goal and at the officials for chalking off a late Junior Hoilett equaliser.

"We've lost four on the trot now and three of them I don't know how we've lost them," a bemused Warnock told reporters on the freezing cold Loftus Road touchline afterwards. On second glance it looked as though Hoilett's goal should have stood, while Warnock was still unhappy with Gary Madine's penalty for Bolton against Cardiff the previous week.

* * * *

Cardiff's luck was out in every sense that Christmas, but January brought new hope in the shape of the mid-season transfer window and the prospect of players returning from injury.

"I think we can have an even better second half to the season, once we have our injured lads back," added Warnock.

It wouldn't have happened, however, without an influx of new players into his squad that January. Warnock was always going to utilise the window – it's not his style to sit back, content with the squad at his disposal. Besides, there was a player he'd had his eye on: the aforementioned Bolton frontman Gary Madine.

Warnock insisted in media interviews that he only wanted to spend on one key player that January. And amid Zohore's struggles, Danny Ward's injury and Bogle's inconsistent form it was obvious that the target would be a marquee striker.

Warnock promised Vincent Tan he wasn't going to spend "silly money".

"There aren't many I want to buy," he said. "Most of the lads I'd like to loan for a few months. It's difficult to buy players in January. There are four or five loan players. If we can get one or two of them, I'd be delighted.

"We're just looking to supplement what we've got with players who I think can do it at this level. There's not a lot wrong."

First in that January were loan signings Yanic Wildschut, a winger from Norwich, and promising Liverpool starlet Marko Grujic, who would be Gunnarsson's midfield replacement.

Then came Nottingham Forest's Jamie Ward in a loan swap deal with Tomlin, with whom Warnock had grown frustrated after the playmaker lost his cool during the defeat to Bolton – and hauled off the substitute after he'd spent just 15 minutes on the field. Reserve left-back Armand Traore was also loaned from Forest, while Liam Feeney's loan from Blackburn was extended.

Sanctioning the departure of Tomlin – a technical but

erratic attacker – and the decision to spend £5million (plus a £1milion add-on if Cardiff were promoted) on Madine were illustrative of Warnock's thinking; results were going to take precedence over anything else. Warnock only wanted players who could play his way.

Madine was a specialist in the air, a solid target man who would suit Cardiff's direct style of play. He was seen as the final piece of Warnock's jigsaw puzzle, his arrival designed to give Zohore the proverbial rocket up the backside with extra competition for his spot.

Of course Warnock needed the backing of Tan and the transfer committee in all of these January deals, though had credit in the bank after the success of summer signings like Etheridge, Mendez-Laing and Callum Paterson.

Tan was rightly concerned about finances, as the club was still clearing debts from its previous Premier League relegation. But having been so successful on a shoestring budget to this point, Warnock felt he deserved to be backed in this January window.

"The transfer committee is happy that Neil understands the financial situation and he is working closely with us on getting the right balance of doing the business we need and conforming with the Financial Fair Play rules," said chief executive Ken Choo at the time.

"Neil is very happy and things are going in the right direction, while the transfer committee and the board here is actively speaking to Vincent on where the club is going, and he is very supportive."

Nathan Blake believes Warnock's shrewd handling of transfers and his experience in keeping to a tight budget was one of the reasons Cardiff hired him in the first place.

He says: "This was a guy who wasn't going to try and sign a level of player which the club couldn't afford, which had happened in previous years. So decisions always have to be taken with the sole interests of the club first."

And yet, something had changed in the space of a year – Cardiff's lofty league position and the prospect of further riches.

With the spectre of the Premier League looming on the horizon, there was little doubt Tan would free up more transfer funds. This was Cardiff's chance and if they could jolt out of their Christmas slumber, promotion was still well within reach.

They had spent more on Madine than on their combined permanent transfers in the summer before, but it was hardly lavish spending in comparison with the financial muscle of Wolves, Fulham and Aston Villa in the Championship that season.

Cardiff felt they were making measured transfer decisions. Agreeing to reject Sheffield Wednesday's offer for Sean Morrison in the summer, the purchase of Madine, the series of incentivised new contracts, these were all indications that Warnock was helping the club put football first.

The commercial side would take care of itself if they reached the promised land of the Premier League.

Besides on the pitch, Cardiff had already begun to return to form that January, thrashing beleaguered Sunderland 4-0 midway through the month, before earning a useful point away at Sheffield Wednesday.

As Warnock now puts it: "As soon as we got out of that run, you knew we were back on track."

He now had the squad he wanted to pursue a place in the Championship top two.

December and January had brought their own challenges. The festivities were over, the finances were in order. From February, it would be all about the football.

CHAPTER NINE

Personal Touch

If modern football has seen the rise of the 'head coach', a role primarily concerned with coaching the team and little else, then there was no doubt there had become fewer old-school 'managers'.

In the case of Neil Warnock's Cardiff City, however – with no director of football and two assistant coaches focussing on the tactical minutiae – the roles were clear. Warnock was a mediator as much as a football manager and his interactions with supporters, players, press and club executives were all of the utmost importance.

Throughout the quest to win promotion, his man-management came to the fore on several occasions and a number of Bluebirds players during that period would cite Warnock as a catalyst for their careers.

He had huge faith in midfielder Joe Ralls, about whom supporters had been unconvinced until Warnock made him a cornerstone of the side. The same could be said of Sean Morrison, who remained Warnock's captain throughout his three-year tenure and whose performance levels increased dramatically under the Yorkshireman.

Lee Peltier had always seemed a 'Warnock player', dependable, committed and fierce in defence, while Bruno Manga was much more consistent with Warnock than under previous managers.

But perhaps three players – and three specific incidents – best exhibit Warnock's ability to change a player's mindset, and therefore their performances for the better.

Kenneth Zohore was a perfect example. The Danish forward had come from nowhere in the latter part of the 2016/17 campaign to make himself Cardiff's number one striker, having been labelled unselectable by the Bluebirds' coaches at the start of that season.

Paul Trollope had initially harboured hopes that Zohore, who spent time on trial at Chelsea as a teenager, would come good.

The former Cardiff boss agreed to turn Zohore's loan from KV Kortrijk – a Belgian club also owned by Vincent Tan – into a permanent deal in the summer of 2016.

Zohore had offered glimpses of his obvious ability in 2015/16, scoring two goals in 12 appearances under Russell Slade.

But keeping him at the club was a gamble. This was a 22-year-old striker who already had a chequered footballing CV, which also included an exciting emergence at FC Copenhagen, a football-less spell at Fiorentina and tours of the Danish and Belgian leagues. He was a Denmark Under-21 international, but he had rarely found consistency.

Cardiff themselves had endured issues with strikers for a number of years. Even when they stormed to the top of the Championship and won promotion in 2012/13, their top scorers were midfielders with modest totals: Aron Gunnarsson and Peter Whittingham with eight apiece. In the intervening years, nobody surpassed a tally of more than 11 for a league campaign and it was infuriating for supporters who just wanted to see goals.

"We've not had a proper goalscorer in the club since Michael Chopra and Jay Bothroyd," says fan Aled Blake, referring to the dynamic strike partnership of the Dave Jones era.

It was an issue that became a festering sore for Bluebirds fans. Where were the reliable goalscorers?

Warnock, upon arrival in October 2016, immediately marked down the centre-forward role as a problem position. He was told by coaches James Rowberry and James McCarthy, who had been there under Trollope, that Zohore was not the answer.

"When we came in we were just about to let Ken Zohore go on a free back to Belgium," says Warnock. "They told us he was no good and everything else."

But Warnock wasn't prepared to give up so easily. He had signed Marouane Chamakh on a free transfer in his first week as manager because he knew he needed a striker – and existing number 9 Rickie Lambert was not going to be the solution.

Neither was Chamakh in the end – he left after three months and never found another professional club. But everyone would get their chance, Warnock decreed.

"We watched him in a couple of practice games and he just had something," he adds on his first impressions of Zohore. "I had a chat with him about him being at the crossroads of his career. I said, 'You've got something you know, but you've got to show it'.

"He had all the attributes to play like I wanted him to play. But I couldn't rule what was inside his head."

Zohore needed guidance. Again for Warnock it was

another Adel Taarabt situation: a player who the manager believed he was the best mentor for, a project that would be the litmus test for the new Cardiff boss' famed man-management skills. Could he be the man who finally got the best from Kenneth Zohore?

Warnock persisted with Lambert for a time, but the arduous Championship fixture schedule was taking its toll on the veteran forward, who struggled to complete 90 minutes every three days. The Bluebirds needed a credible alternative, someone with Lambert's physicality but more energy to go with it.

After a few weeks of solid training, Warnock ushered Zohore into the fray on a cold December night at home to Wolves.

Matt Doherty's long range shot had given the hosts an early 1-0 lead, with Cardiff struggling to gain a foothold in the contest as Anthony Pilkington led the forward line. Lambert and Zohore were both on the bench and, at half-time, Warnock turned to the young Dane.

"The crowd were trying to help us but it was a cold night," remembers Warnock. "Ken was on the bench and we didn't look like scoring."

Warnock collared Zohore into the changing room's shower area, the only place available for the private one-to-one discussion that needed to take place, and told the striker this was his do-or-die moment. Having not even featured under Warnock before, the Cardiff manager was now pinning his hopes on Zohore. He trusted his player's ability, it was merely a case of mindset.

Warnock adds: "I was leant on a wheelie bin in the shower and I said, 'Listen Ken, this is it for you' and he said, 'What do you mean, gaffer?' and I said, 'This next 45 minutes will decide whether you stay here or whether you go, because I've had enough of you, this hasn't been good enough'.

"I said, 'I'm gonna put you on now for 45 minutes and I'm not bothered if you have a stinker, I want you to cause havoc and run and die for me like you've never done in your life, because it's not just for me, it's for your future, this, do you understand?'

"And he said yes and his eyes were bright and clear and he went out and did what nobody else thought he could do, it was like a miracle. At that time it was so crucial for him because he just hadn't fulfilled his potential."

Zohore was a revelation. He never stopped running and changed the pace of the game, as Cardiff came from behind to win 2-1 thanks to goals from Pilkington and Matt Connolly.

Warnock could sense something stirring in Zohore that night. It was his eureka moment.

The Dane scored his first goal under Warnock a fortnight later, in a belligerent display at Brentford, before embarking on a remarkable scoring streak from the final day of January until 1st April.

He scored 10 goals in 11 games, one of them a stunning solo effort against Preston, and finished the season as Cardiff's top scorer with 12.

It wasn't an entirely prolific total to compete with Bothroyd or Chopra of yesteryear, but for a player who had been discarded and tossed on the scrapheap midway through the campaign, it was a fine effort.

"There was not a player here like that when I came here," Warnock reflected towards the end of that season. "He was not a waste of time, but he wasn't far away from being a waste of time. He walked about, wouldn't tackle, wouldn't chase back and he wore gloves everywhere.

"The minimum you should get out of a player is 100 per cent. Then the ability goes on top. You need that work ethic at any level of the game.

"When you do that, you make your own luck, as [golfing legend] Gary Player used to say."

That ethos summed up Warnock's management style,

Warnock is unveiled as the new Cardiff City boss in October 2016, alongside chairman Mehmet Dalman, who'd prove a supportive figure throughout his reign.

Back at Loftus Road with the Bluebirds, and Warnock shows the QPR fans present that he's still got the magic touch...

Mission accomplished: Warnock seals promotion to the big time in May 2018, at the climax of his first full season in the Cardiff hotseat.

Sean Morrison was the goalscoring hero against Hull to help seal promotion glory.

Clockwise from left: Warnock pictured with wife Sharon, vice-captain Sol Bamba and Bluebirds owner Vincent Tan; in their own differing ways, three pivotal figures throughout his Cardiff reign. Below: A Bluebirds fan sends his own message to Tottenham over their potential managerial vacancy.

Hands off Warnock

when Poch goes

Man Utd

Spanish loan signing Victor Camarasa
was a revelation in the top flight;
he was the goalscoring hero against
Leicester City over the festive period,
much to the delight of his manager.

Warnock credited Sharon's decision to move to South Wales as a key factor in his successes at the club, including this win over Brighton (below) to give them hope of survival.

The city of Cardiff is stunned by the death of Emiliano Sala in January 2019. Supporters came in their droves to pay their respects and tributes to a life cut tragically short.

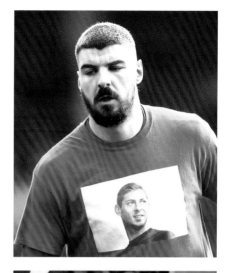

Callum Paterson shows
off the players' tribute
to Sala ahead of the
clash with Southampton
at St Mary's, while
supporters continued to
show their feelings for
the fallen star.

Farewell to the Premier League in style as Nathaniel Mendez-Laing's double sees off Manchester United and former Bluebirds boss Ole Gunnar Solskjaer at Old Trafford.

which had been personified on the pitch by the revitalised Zohore. He demanded full-blooded commitment from his players in every game and the penny had now dropped for the Danish forward.

But whereas in Zohore Warnock found a player whose entire mentality needed transforming, Sol Bamba appeared to be the ideal mentee.

Bamba, having turned 32, knew he was in the autumn of his career and wanted to waste no time in working to achieve a lifelong dream: to play in the Premier League. He trained as he played – with determination and industry – and Warnock loved his attitude.

Yet on a seemingly insignificant Saturday at Ipswich's Portman Road in December 2016, three days before Zohore's Wolves epiphany, Bamba would test Warnock's man-management skills in an entirely different way.

Cardiff were meandering towards a solid 1-1 draw with Ipswich when Bamba reacted angrily to a challenge from Jonathan Douglas. What happened next was quite incredible and completely out of character.

After going down following the collision, Bamba sprang up to his feet, pushing the Cardiff physiotherapist – who had come onto the pitch to treat him – down to the ground and running to confront the Ipswich players.

The Bluebirds, playing in red that night, were quickly reduced to 10 men by referee James Adcock. And Bamba saw the red mist descend, pushing and shoving his own manager on the sideline – with Warnock desperately trying to restrain him.

Bamba would later describe the incident as "a moment of craziness" as he was banned for four matches. Warnock, having brought Bamba to Cardiff and invested so much time and energy in a player he believed was perfect for his management, felt understandably let down.

"That's the worst thing that's ever happened to me in my football career," Bamba says now.

"Because of the relationship I had with the manager and it just wasn't me. I lost my head. It's not an excuse, it was a bad tackle before and I've been in games before when I've had arguments or fights but I've never ever reacted the way I did that day.

"That's one of my lowest moments. And I've got kids and it was a bad example. I'm always looking to be a role model and set a good example because I know how many people are watching. It wasn't acceptable and I still feel bad about it."

How Warnock dealt with the incident would be intriguing.

After the game, a furious Warnock told journalists: "He is distraught in the dressing room and quite rightly. For me, he is one of the best in the Championship and that was a blemish I haven't seen in his make-up"

And after admonishing Bamba so publicly, some believed the relationship between manager and player was irreparable.

But the Ivorian reveals the conversations he held with Warnock in the aftermath of the incident were akin to those that might occur between a headmaster and his misbehaving prefect. The defender was too influential to be cast aside, Warnock knew that. Bamba would be back.

"It was another example of Neil's man-management probably being the best in the business," explains Bamba.

"When we finished the game and went into the dressing room, he just said to me, 'We're going to sort this out on Monday'."

It would be a weekend of quiet reflection for both men. Bamba explains: "And on Monday morning he brought me into his office and said to me, 'I'm not even angry, I'm disappointed'.

"That was the worst for me, I remember my mum and dad used to say that. I would have preferred him to be angry and I just didn't know what to say. All I could do was say, 'It won't happen again and I'm going to do my best to repay you'.

"But he didn't make a big meal of it."

The incident would eventually become a running joke between the pair, because it was such an anomaly for an otherwise exemplary player. A blot on his copybook.

And since Warnock was building his Cardiff squad around leaders like Bamba, he maintained his routine of inviting the defender into his personal office at the Vale Resort training ground – after a short exile.

"For the next couple of days it was a bit funny for me," adds the Ivorian.

"We always had loads of jokes together and he'd regularly ask me to come into his office and have a chat about anything – our kids, just life in general. But that didn't happen for a couple of days and I thought he was upset with me.

"So he made me feel he was disappointed for a while but thankfully it went back to normal. Even when I speak to Neil about it now I feel bad. He always reminded me about it whenever I started to feel angry."

The Bamba incident and the rise of Zohore were two contrasting and very early challenges for Warnock's man-management skills at Cardiff. But in the 2017/18 campaign, there would be more hurdles for him to overcome, obstacles that might otherwise derail a team's tilt at promotion.

* * * *

In February 2018, after recovering from their winter blip, Cardiff faced the unstoppable force of runaway Premier League leaders Manchester City in the FA Cup fourth round. After needing a replay to edge past Mansfield Town in the previous round, it was a rich reward for Warnock's side.

The game was billed a test of their top-flight credentials, an almighty challenge against the country's best team and a great occasion for a sold-out Cardiff City Stadium to savour. Unfortunately for the Bluebirds and their reputation in the wider footballing world, they made headlines for all the wrong reasons in a 2-0 defeat to Pep Guardiola's side.

Joe Bennett was vilified in the national media for a horrendous tackle on Man City's Leroy Sane, for which he was only given a yellow card – before receiving a second yellow later in the game. The names of Bennett and Cardiff were tarnished, for a time, with Warnock's players branded "thugs" and Guardiola calling for greater protection from referees.

Even Sane's international side Germany got involved on social media, telling Cardiff "please don't hurt our players" with a World Cup imminent. The club were public enemy number one.

There was no doubt some of the criticism was harsh, as Bennett issued a heartfelt apology, insisting: "I didn't mean to catch him like I did."

But Warnock, clearly fearful that his players could gain an unwanted – and unfair – reputation as a rough team, could not defend Bennett. While he admitted the left-back was not malicious, he described the player's conduct in the FA Cup tie "pathetic" and "disrespectful to teammates", as the red card saw Bennett suspended for crucial league games.

Cardiff had turned to Armand Traore, whose January signing was designed to bring Bennett some competition for his left-back slot. Before the Man City game, Bennett had been in decent form, but Traore's arrival was timely.

He came into the side during Bennett's suspension, starring in a thumping 4-1 win at Leeds United and then scoring a vital goal in a 2-0 victory over Bolton at home.

Bennett faced a long road back, not just to restore his reputation but to regain his spot. Warnock had even forced him to train in isolation – and while other players were enjoying a break – in the wake of his Manchester City red card.

You could call the treatment harsh, and in comparison with Warnock's handling of Zohore and Bamba, it was. But it worked.

"I didn't mind, it was something I had to do, a bit of discipline," said Bennett. He came back stronger, solidifying his place in the side and contributing to the Bluebirds' 11-game unbeaten run in spring 2018.

What does Warnock's respective treatment of Zohore, Bamba and Bennett tell us about his man-management style? That he treats every case and every player on an individual basis? Certainly. Also that he deals with the person as well as the footballer by speaking to their own ambitions and desires.

It's no coincidence that so many of Warnock's former players speak so effusively about playing under him; and that he still reunites with members of his former promotion-winning Scarborough, Huddersfield, Plymouth Argyle, Notts County and Sheffield United sides decades after leaving.

After hanging up his boots as a player aged 30, Warnock started his managerial career by taking charge of a Sunday league team in Todwick near Sheffield, washing the kit himself every weekend, before landing a job at non-league Gainsborough Trinity in 1980. He had his own chiropody practice and is also a fully-qualified referee.

His journey up the managerial ladder struck a chord with so many players because they knew he'd got there on merit, after being – by his own admission – an average but effective player in the lower leagues.

His former Hartlepool manager Len Ashurst was his greatest inspiration and Warnock vowed to put his players first when he stepped into management.

"The pleasing thing for me when I look back on my career is that 95 per cent of the players who played for me will have good memories of it," says Warnock.

"That's all you can do as a manager, unless you're blessed with one of these top clubs with unlimited funds.

"They've got diplomas for football management now at universities and all that, but it's still mostly how you deal with people, how you get the best out of them at every level. And that's not going to change and I enjoy that. I enjoy seeing average players become good players. And good players becoming great players."

By the end of March 2018, it was clear Warnock had turned Cardiff City from an average Championship team into a good one, who now stood on the brink of promotion. But despite the momentum they had accrued in that period after January and the Man City game, he would continue to face challenges to his man-management before the Bluebirds could dream of the Premier League.

CHAPTER TEN

Push Your Luck

Despite the advent of tactical analysis, marginal gains and exhaustive preparation routines, superstition remains rife in professional football.

It appears counter-intuitive in a sport increasingly dependent on science and data, yet even those with decades of experience in the game believe luck plays its part. Tempting fate is a big 'no no'.

So when Cardiff City fan, former player and pundit Nathan Blake hosted his weekly Blakey's Bootroom podcast for *WalesOnline* during the Bluebirds 2018 promotion run-in, he refused to ever say definitively whether his beloved team would accomplish their aims.

Even Neil Warnock himself is known to adhere to some bizarres superstitions, especially in the period before a game when he becomes terribly beset by nerves. Former Huddersfield striker Andy Booth once recalled the time when Warnock suspended training because a solitary magpie flew onto the pitch. "One magpie is unlucky, we've got to wait for another one before we start training again," Warnock is reported to have said.

Other well-known Warnock superstitions include wearing the same suit for matches, using the same razor blade until his team were beaten and refusing to use the toilet until his players are on the pitch before a game. He once claimed in a 2007 interview that he kept to more than 300 superstitions.

Inspired by managerial idol Brian Clough's habit of writing 'be good' in his match programme notes, Warnock finished his own fortnightly message to home supporters by saying, 'Take care and be lucky'.

"I thought I can't put 'be good' because there's only one Cloughie, so I'll put 'be lucky'," says Warnock.

It spoke to that superstitious side of him and was magnified as Cardiff were chasing promotion. Tension can do funny things to the minds of professional footballers, though sports psychologist Dr Richard Lustberg revealed these pseudo-sciences are no bad thing for sports stars.

"Superstitions are a coping mechanism to deal with the

pressure to succeed," he said. Athletes begin to believe – they, in fact, want to believe – that their routine of choice is enhancing their performance. In reality, it is just practice and confidence that make them perform better."

Maybe Sol Bamba was aware of Lustberg's theory. Because while Warnock and Blake were fearful of tempting fate, the Cardiff centre-back was outwardly confident. He had a justified faith in the Bluebirds' approach and, while appearing as a guest on the Bootroom podcast alongside Blake, stated that he believed promotion would be won. There were still nine games of the season to be played.

How could he be so sure?

"The first minute I got to Cardiff, seeing the players that were at the club and the ones coming in, I honestly thought to myself that if we got enough good results, steadied the ship, we could push for promotion the next season," says Bamba.

"We had a manager who'd done it before, a good group of players, we just needed one or two additions and we'd be fine.

"I said to the lads when I arrived, 'You don't realise how good you are,' and I'd been in the Championship for a long time. I thought we shouldn't just be looking to be safe, we should be looking for promotion next season.

"What we did then was build the foundations. We got used to the way the manager wanted to play, got a few more additions. Funnily enough, that's exactly what happened and the season we went up I was always convinced we'd do it.

"For some reason I had a feeling we'd be okay and thank God we managed to do it."

Bamba's confidence was no doubt a product of his belief in Warnock's methods. Because while the manager occasionally doubted himself, his senior players never did.

Sean Morrison was similarly adamant that it would happen, as he said in an interview around the same time, in March. "If we stick to what we're doing, I'm sure we'll be fine," said the captain.

Warnock's chief enforcers, his valued centre-back duo, were reinforcing the message; Cardiff were now promotion favourites for a very good reason.

The skipper had a point to prove, however, after he'd risked destabilising the entire campaign with one moment of madness; a video leaked onto social media of Morrison in the back of car launching a foul-mouthed verbal tirade mocking Derby County players Richard Keogh, Alex Pearce and Jason Shackell.

The language was unsavoury – Morrison calling Keogh

"shit at football" – and a bad look for the club. It was understood the video was intended as a private joke between the players on their own WhatApp group, yet had been shared all over Twitter. It left Warnock with questions to answer.

The context to the video was the postponed match between Derby and Cardiff, originally scheduled for Sunday 18th March but called off due to unseasonal snow, the so-called 'Beast from the East'.

Morrison claimed in the video, "You're all scared of playing us" – and Warnock can now reveal Derby did exaggerate the amount of snow around Pride Park that day, with boss Gary Rowett concerned at the time that his long injury list would mean almost certain defeat for the Rams.

"That week was probably the biggest test of my career because Mozza had let me down really, as my captain, getting involved with this video tape with the Derby County players," says Warnock.

"Ever since, by the way, Rowett did tell me they got it called off. I asked him to tell me the truth and he said, 'Oh aye, we'd got so many injuries'.

"It was funny as they shovelled all the snow into one pile and took pictures from behind the snow and put it out – there were only two piles, and we knew they had stitched us up. We'd have beaten them and [Rowett] knew that, he's said that."

At the time Cardiff didn't have enough evidence – though it didn't stop Bluebirds fans and players calling furiously for a Football League investigation. They felt wronged and that feeling of frustration had manifested itself in the Morrison video.

* * * *

Warnock was left with another mess to clean up. He claimed in his next press conference that his Cardiff squad had videos on their phones of Derby players saying far worse.

But to continue the feud, he knew, would have been counter-productive to his side's promotion hopes.

They hadn't got the chance to beat Derby when they wanted to, but they remained in the box seat for promotion, despite the fact Fulham were romping to win after win in the hunt for second place.

Warnock may be superstitious, but he still backed his players' ability – Morrison included – to hold their nerve. He needed stability on the pitch, so he stuck by his captain.

Cardiff beat Burton 3-1 at home to head into April in a strong position, before a last-gasp Anthony Pilkington equaliser three days later at Sheffield United – in a game that the Blades had utterly dominated – felt like another boost. The Morrison controversy quickly became old news, though the next five fixtures looked hugely daunting: Wolves, Aston Villa, Norwich, Nottingham Forest and… the rearranged game against Derby.

Warnock would need to call upon that much-vaunted unity once again during this period. It had served Cardiff well at the start of the season and they'd stuck together throughout their Christmas struggles, an uncertain January and through the Bennett and Morrison incidents.

"This was on another level to anything I've ever seen and it speaks volumes to have that unity off the pitch – and you naturally take that onto the pitch," says Greg Halford.

This is when, despite the togetherness, Cardiff's performances often became disjointed and stodgy. Fatigue and pressure meant they could no longer find their free-flowing best, but the Pilkington leveller at Bramall Lane proved they would fight until the end.

"We weren't the best team in the league, we didn't have the best players," Halford adds. "But we had this unity and this never-say-die attitude that got us promoted."

The clash with Wolves at Cardiff City Stadium on 6th April, another Friday night game and another firecracker atmosphere, was enormous.

A record league crowd for the stadium of 29,317 witnessed second host first, with Cardiff gunning to close the deficit to just three points with a game in hand.

The match followed a similar pattern to the Molineux meeting between the sides in August, with Wolves dominating possession but Cardiff still able to carve out clear cut chances on the break.

Nuno Espirito Santo's team was, bar two players, identical to the one he'd picked earlier in the campaign, while Warnock was able to call upon Callum Paterson, Craig Bryson and Yanic Wildschut.

Ruben Neves and Diogo Jota had mastered the Championship by this stage in the season, however, and the former drilled a 25-yard free-kick into the top corner to seemingly secure the points in the 67th minute.

A win for Wolves would have virtually guaranteed them automatic promotion and left Cardiff under pressure in second.

But the Bluebirds kept fighting and, in dramatic late scenes, substitute Gary Madine won a penalty – and had the chance to convert his first Cardiff goal from the spot. John Ruddy saved miraculously, before the home side were awarded a second stoppage-time penalty by referee Mike Dean, when the fit-again Aron Gunnarsson was tripped in the box.

Joe Ralls had been on penalty duties for Warnock's side since Peter Whittingham's departure, but he was missing with injury. Junior Hoilett stepped up this time with the chance to salvage a point with the second spot-kick. Crossbar. Defeat for Cardiff.

The aftermath of the 1-0 win for Wolves will go down in Championship folklore for the memorable row that ensued afterwards between Warnock and Nuno. The Bluebirds boss was incensed that his opposite number had raced onto the pitch to celebrate with Ruddy rather than shake his hand. When Nuno belatedly went to apologise, Warnock walked away angrily, repeatedly telling him to "fuck off" on the pitch.

The cameras had their juicy footage while in the tunnel afterwards, Warnock rejected Nuno's further attempts to smooth things over.

"You're not going to get happy faces," Warnock told

the media afterwards. It was the understatement of the century. He was seething.

Many claims have since been made about Warnock and Nuno's supposedly frosty relationship, but the Cardiff boss was among the first to text his congratulations to the Wolves boss when their promotion had been sealed. At the LMA dinner to conclude the 2017/18 season the pair again chatted amicably and still hold each other in high esteem.

Yet their on-field row was a sign of the bubbling tensions. And again Cardiff had to haul themselves off the canvas, especially after a disappointing midweek trip to Aston Villa yielded another painful 1-0 defeat, this time to a late Jack Grealish stunner.

To win no points from such knife-edge games against promotion rivals left a bitter taste in the mouth and Cardiff briefly found themselves in third, below Fulham, albeit with a match in hand. But as Bamba now says: "After that, we were more dogged – we had to dig in and win games 1-0."

Digging deep was the realm of both the players and manager. Losing close games was very unlike Cardiff under Warnock but, as always, they produced a response, beating Norwich and Nottingham Forest by narrow margins in successive weeks. It would have been so easy to crack but as Aled Blake remembers the sheer force of Warnock's personality was helping the Bluebirds over the line in each game.

The manager's determination to win an eighth career promotion, to prove the doubters wrong and to give Cardiff supporters what they craved, underpinned everything that happened in that thrilling season finale.

"I think it had to happen, it couldn't *not* have happened," says Blake on promotion.

"As a person and a manager he had such a will to succeed at the club. It was such a big personal record for him. The promotion run-in felt like the final part of a long journey that we'd been on.

"It sounds cliched, but it was a bit like that, a crystallisation of Warnock's work in knitting the fans back together and creating a togetherness at the club."

It would have been the perfect fairytale for Warnock had Cardiff gone back to Pride Park on 24th April for the rescheduled contest and beaten Derby. It wasn't to be. Rowett's men were better prepared this time, with many of their injured stars available again. They won 3-1.

"I thought we played alright that night but we had so much on with that game being called off and the videos," says Warnock. "I remember Cameron Jerome scoring a couple and somebody that I knew was up in the lounge after the game.

"Apparently Jerome went up there with the owner, Mel Morris, to be presented with the man of the match. And the compere says to him, 'Looks very good for the play-offs now, who would you want in the play-offs?' and he said, 'I wouldn't mind this lot, Cardiff.'

"It was us or Fulham and everyone said Fulham were going to steamroller us – they'd said it for six to eight weeks. And they should have done. They had the best squad by a mile.

"I texted Mel Morris and said, 'Well I hope I disappoint you'. That made me more determined."

Jerome, a former Cardiff striker, had lit the blue touch paper and Cardiff had one more season-defining performance in them to seal an automatic promotion place at Fulham's expense.

There would be nothing lucky about it.

CHAPTER ELEVEN

Blue Skies

Standing between Cardiff City and the Premier League, between Neil Warnock and a record eighth career promotion was one fixture – the game Warnock now calls his most memorable in football management.

After all the twists and turns of the 2017/18 campaign, it would all come down to a single Saturday afternoon at Hull City.

Cardiff, by this stage, were under severe pressure. Despite the victories over Norwich and Nottingham Forest – which had both been secured with late winners – they travelled to Humberside needing three points to keep control of their own destiny.

Fulham played Sunderland in the Friday night fixture that week and, after falling 1-0 behind, somehow squeezed through 2-1 against the Championship's bottom club with the winner coming from their January loan signing, striker Aleksandar Mitrovic. Slavisa Jokanovic's men had enjoyed several slices of luck at Craven Cottage that night, as a despondent Bluebirds squad watched on television from their Hull hotel.

"We watched them and how Sunderland didn't win that game, I still don't know," says Warnock.

"They had a certain penalty that the ref didn't give them, the officials gave Fulham everything and they somehow managed to win."

Fulham had done their bit and the win lifted them back into second place, two points ahead of Cardiff and with a superior goal difference.

The Tigers, spearheaded by a player who'd had unsuccessful trials at Cardiff as a child – forward Jarrod Bowen – had stopped Derby, Aston Villa and Fulham from winning on their home patch that season. Despite their lowly league position of 18th, they were in good form, having lost just two of their previous 12.

To beat Hull at the KCom Stadium, Cardiff would need to call upon their reserves of energy, determination and that famous team spirit. They had also devised a specific strategy to stop Bowen, who was among the league's top scorers with 14 goals. Warnock's men had been stung earlier that week by the 3-1 defeat at Derby, but this game would be more akin to the Norwich trip two weeks earlier, in which they had rallied late on against mid-table opposition – thanks to a key half-time pep talk from the manager.

Sol Bamba reveals the Cardiff boss used this tense moment, with their clash at Carrow Road locked at 0-0, to inject a little humour to proceedings.

"We were playing away at Norwich and I came off with a groin injury after about half an hour," says Bamba, who was replaced by Bruno Manga.

"I was in the dressing room, upset that I'd come off, but before I came off I did a tackle and played a diagonal forward to try and play through Mendez-Laing. But I messed it up, it got intercepted, they counter-attacked and nearly scored. And I had to make a tackle which then meant I had to come off."

Bamba, who had flared up an injury that he'd been nursing all season, was then taken aback when Warnock began to deal him a hammering in the dressing room at half-time.

He adds: "The gaffer said to me, 'Why are you trying to be clever? You could have just passed it simply. You lost the ball and then you had to run 40 yards, make a tackle and you've done your groin!'

"We had a huge argument. He shouted at me, 'Get out of my face, you can't help the team anyway'.

"So after a few swear words I went in the shower and after that his face changed. He was dying laughing and said, 'See lads, that's why we're going to win the game, I need that kind of character and commitment!'

"And the lads went out and won the game 2-0. And I didn't even know about this until after and the players told me he did that on purpose, because we were flat in the first half and needed motivating – and that's the gaffer all over."

At half-time at Hull two weeks later, Cardiff were in a stronger position, 1-0 up thanks to Sean Morrison's headed opener and two despairing defensive blocks by Bamba, who was playing on despite his groin niggle.

The Bluebirds had been heroic all over the pitch, though their performance came as something of a surprise to Warnock, who had overseen a tough few days in training beforehand. The disappointment of the Derby defeat had punctured the mood somewhat.

"I remember that week we were a little bit subdued when we had a session," says Warnock.

"We talked a bit about Hull City as they had Bowen and we wanted to work on restricting their wide lads and give our players more opportunities.

"But really it wasn't anything physical, it was the end of the season and we didn't need any physical stuff. It was just a talk to say, 'Listen, we haven't done all this to let it go, everyone in the country thinks Fulham are gonna do us'."

Morrison took the message to heart more than most, enjoying arguably his best ever performance in a Cardiff shirt. He capped it with a remarkable second goal, racing forward in the 80th minute to seal the win.

Warnock, to this day, still wonders how the centre-back managed to storm into the box to latch onto Nathaniel Mendez-Laing's pass and slot home left-footed with the composure of a top striker.

But at the time, he didn't care. The away end erupted, as a tousle-haired Morrison slid towards them on his knees and thumped the Cardiff badge on his chest. It's an image now ingrained in the memories of Bluebirds fans and Warnock.

He couldn't be prouder of his players. And the fact captain Morrison had bounced back from the Derby video fiasco to single-handedly inspire this vital win was so significant. The togetherness had lasted the distance: from Devon and Cornwall, up and down the country for 45 games, to the banks of the River Humber.

"I know we're limited and not everybody's cup of tea but we're not going away, we're like a rash," Warnock said, beaming after the game. "I'm ever so proud of them, they just don't know when they're beat."

The win lifted Cardiff to 89 points with one game remaining. They would host Reading on the season's final day while Fulham, on 88 points, travelled to Birmingham City's St Andrews.

The job wasn't quite finished, yet Warnock somehow felt sure his players had done the hard part. They wouldn't relinquish this.

Warnock says: "I know winning promotion is a lovely feeling, but [that game] at Hull City epitomised my whole career as a manager; how to overcome adversity when everyone writes you off and how to instil that mentality into a group of players.

"It was one of the best weeks of my career to get a win and a performance like that after such a disappointment against Derby County."

It felt appropriate that Cardiff's season had built to a crescendo, with the biggest home crowd of the season,

32,478, packing into Cardiff City Stadium for the denouement against Reading. Only 1,700 away fans had been able to witness Cardiff's season opener at Burton Albion nine months earlier and even fewer saw the pre-season games at Tavistock and Bodmin. They had come a long way.

* * * *

In the end, the only goals the Bluebirds fans got to cheer on the final day of the campaign were scored by Birmingham, as word filtered through via phones, radios and the media contingent's laptops that Fulham had fallen 1-0 behind at St Andrews – and then 2-0.

While Cardiff's clash with Reading remained goalless and largely uneventful, there was a bizarre outpouring of joy thanks to unseen first half goals from Lukas Jutkiewicz and home skipper Harlee Dean.

The noises were unlike any normal goal celebrations, slowly rippling around the crowd as the realisation dawned. The goals belonged to Cardiff as much as they did to Birmingham, who saw out a 3-1 win.

On a sweltering hot May afternoon, Cardiff City

Stadium was a cauldron ready to boil over. And towards the end of the 0-0 draw, it nearly did, as one or two premature celebrators stormed the pitch before the final whistle.

When it eventually came, the Bluebirds' jubilation knew no bounds. A sea of blue quickly engulfed the green turf: flares went up, flags were flown, the volume was louder than anything heard at the stadium before. Players were mobbed, hugged, kissed.

Yet the newspaper back pages the next day and the viral videos on social media could only tell half the story. The atmosphere was unique in its euphoria. Only football can make you feel like this.

They say you shouldn't compare eras, but the Cardiff fans had no shame in their belief that this was so much sweeter than before because blue was the colour. Aled Blake was there, on the pitch with the rest of them – as he was five years before – and the differences with the previous promotion in 2013 were clear.

"That promotion and the feel about the club then was of one of a joyous sense of relief," says Blake.

"Relief because of all the ill-feeling and upset that we'd had in the seasons before, which had been swept away by Warnock and his work in bringing us together again as a fanbase. The last time we had a Premier League promotion, it was a bittersweet moment.

"It's hard to get away from cliches when you talk about football but it was bittersweet because there was something not quite right about it: the fact the players were all in red, there was this divided fanbase. We were happy to see the club going up but there was something jarring about it.

"The Reading match and the celebrations after it was an unbridled unfurling of pleasure and relief and joy – all sorts of emotions."

And for all the brilliance of Warnock and the achievement of his own personal record, plus the dedication and determination of a truly special squad, it felt like a promotion that belonged to supporters.

Their loyalty had finally been rewarded. They could celebrate without worry, toasting the future and savouring the present.

They could hoist aloft Vincent Tan on their shoulders and serenade Warnock knowing that they'd won promotion the Cardiff way: upsetting the odds, with a team and manager who possessed heart and soul and – most importantly – wearing their true blue colours.

"It reminded me of the promotions we used to have as

a kid, when the fans ran onto the pitch at Ninian Park," says Aled Blake, referencing the promoted Cardiff teams of 1988, 1993, 1999, 2001 and 2003.

"It was an uninhibited celebration and I think a lot of the jubilation was a release of tensions that had been built up in the previous years.

"We can make too much of the whole 'red' thing and the way the club had been run before but when you think about it that was a really divided time, the fans were fed up, Tan had lost interest – and then Warnock came along and he brought the fun back to watching Cardiff City."

The sun-soaked celebrations would carry on throughout the day, as clusters of Cardiff fans paraded around the city singing about Junior Hoilett, Sean Morrison and Aron Gunnarsson.

For the players, too, the revelry would continue long into the night, as the club held its end of season awards party at the city centre Mercure Hotel, with Morrison winning the main prize.

"Where do I start? It's been a season to remember," said the centre-back, collecting the player of the season award.

He'd beaten Bamba by one per cent in the vote, thanks to his talismanic display at Hull. Hoilett was named player's year of the year, Callum Paterson the best young player, while Bamba's stunning strike at Brentford won goal of the season.

"Every single one of the boys has had my back since the start of the year and it's been a rollercoaster all year," added Morrison. "I need to thank all the boys. What can I say? It's been incredible and today has been a day none of us will ever forget. It's been amazing."

Morrison and Bamba then led the dancing at the unofficial after-party in city centre nightclub Tiger Tiger, where Hoilett shared around the champagne and Paterson brought out his trademark dance routines from the video game *Fortnite*. Old Cardiff heroes like Kevin McNaughton, who had travelled down to Wales to see their former side complete the job, joined in.

Players' wives and girlfriends were there too, though by that stage Warnock had retreated home. He would address fans officially a week later outside Cardiff Castle following a glorious promotion bus parade through the city streets.

After taking calls from friends and family, giving the media their reaction interviews, and accepting the jubilation alongside Tan, Mehmet Dalman, Ken Choo and his players in the stands – lifting the trophy that said the Bluebirds were promoted – there was time for some quiet reflection. "People take a lot for granted in football and some people don't get a lot of credit," said Warnock, in his parting message at the awards dinner. "There are so many unsung heroes."

So as Warnock made his way to his house in Ogmore-by-Sea with wife Sharon that night, he knew he couldn't have done it without her, his ultimate unsung star.

Sharon gave him unwavering support whatever had happened on the pitch, but her breast cancer diagnosis in November 2015 had put football into stark perspective for Warnock. Back then, in semi-retirement, his focus was on caring for his wife. The idea of managing a side to promotion was far from his thoughts.

He admits that Sharon pushed him back into management, joking that she had become irritated by him "skulking around the house" in Cornwall and told him, in no uncertain terms, to accept the job offer from Rotherham in February 2016.

The transition to Cardiff was easy then, with Warnock quickly moving into a house away from the city centre glare and Sharon deciding she wanted to live with her husband in Ogmore, rather than drive up for weekly visits.

She offered the home support that he would call upon

time and time again during such a tumultuous season. "The plus was Sharon, she just loved it," says Warnock.

"She loved the fans, talking to them. We used to go Waitrose in Cowbridge and wherever we went I'd be stopped for photographs and Sharon would take the photos for them. People would think, 'He's only ordinary him, doing a trolley shop'.

"I loved it too, Ogmore-by-Sea, wow. Just to get away from football was great. I knew Sharon would come with me. Sharon just had a feeling about Cardiff, I've never known her like that.

"Within about two months, when I got the house she came up a few times and one time she said, 'I'm going to come up and stop with you'.

"Everything was great because when she's around, it's so much better for me. We used to go walking the dogs out on the beach, it was fabulous."

Bluebirds fans had rightly viewed Warnock as their messiah on that summer's day, yet there was no doubt Sharon Warnock had played her own role in Cardiff City's promotion. The club owed plenty to her quiet reassuring voice.

So as the sun set on the club's most famous day and the Premier League beckoned, Warnock could bask in a brief sense of satisfaction. There would be uncertainty ahead, Warnock knew that, but just for a moment it felt like the clouds had lifted.

CHAPTER TWELVE

Bright Side

Sir Alex Ferguson and many of his former Manchester United stars readily admitted they didn't enjoy their trophy wins as much as they should have. Roy Keane, speaking as a pundit on Sky Sports years after that golden period at Old Trafford, admitted he wished he'd savoured the victories a little more, that he had relaxed from time to time.

"I couldn't think that way, that was my mindset and I was never happy really," said Keane.

For Ferguson and his players it was about quickly shifting the focus onto next season, and the next objective. Have you won the league? Fine, now plan how to win it better next season. Enjoying the moment was a brief and rare luxury.

There's no doubt this relentless mentality has worked for a number of elite managers – and speaks to the work ethic that makes them so successful.

And even though Neil Warnock was desperate to savour the glory of May 2018 and allow himself a period of down time after winning promotion with Cardiff City, he couldn't help but think about the job ahead. Such is the mind of a top manager.

He had smiled and laughed throughout the open-top bus parade that took place on Sunday 13th May, the week after the Reading game. That jubilant journey saw Cardiff's players ferried from their stadium, on the borders of Leckwith, Canton and Grangetown, through packed streets into the heart of the city – reflecting their journey from obscurity back to relevance under Warnock. Another glorious day.

But the manager's final act before the summer break was to address the massed Bluebirds supporters in a brief speech in front of Cardiff Castle, where the parade reached its climax. After toasting the triumphant season that had gone before, Warnock finished by sending a warning about what was to come. The Premier League was in the back of his mind.

"We're going to give it our best shot next year, make no

mistake," he said to the Cardiff fans. "All you lot have got to help us from the very start. When we lose four on the trot, I don't want any [chants of] 'Warnock out!'

"Just remember where you were when I first came here, alright? Thanks everybody and see you next year."

And with that, the promotion celebrations were over. They would always be savoured, especially by the fans, but it was quite clear the minds of Warnock and his staff were already putting together their blueprint for 2018/19. The supporters had been told to expect a bumpy ride, though if he wanted a smoother transition into the top flight, Warnock knew that summer would be pivotal.

In his 2013 book *Gaffer,* Warnock famously said: "People think football managers have the summer off. I wish."

At the time, he was talking about Queens Park Rangers' chaotic summer of 2011, immediately after they had won promotion. Back then, he knew his QPR side needed major surgery and sought a number of transfer deals to get his squad prepared for the Premier League – as he would later do with Cardiff.

But there was a problem; Bernie Ecclestone and Flavio Briatore wanted to sell the club and so were unwilling to grant Warnock the necessary funds for transfers. The

Yorkshireman spoke of his frustration as a number of deals were refused by the owners, before a last-gasp sale of the club to Malaysian air magnate Tony Fernandes prompted a deadline day trolley dash.

Warnock signed Joey Barton, Shaun Wright-Phillips, Anton Ferdinand, Luke Young, Armand Traore and Jason Puncheon for around £10million combined in the final week of the window, having only spent £1.25million in the seven weeks before.

It was a horrifically stressful time for Warnock, who revealed that he'd joked with his wife about being sacked by QPR – it felt like a case of 'when' not 'if'. The turbulence at Loftus Road that summer was no way to prepare for a campaign in the world's toughest league and it showed, as they lost their season opener 4-0 at home to Bolton and Warnock – having stormed to the top of the Championship the previous year – soon found himself under pressure.

He was relieved of his duties midway through the Rs' Premier League season as the club felt they were at risk of relegation.

Warnock has long endured a strained relationship with the Premier League, dating back to the sour moment his Sheffield United side were relegated on the final day of the 2006/07 season, thanks largely to West Ham's Carlos Tevez. The Hammers had broken rules on third-party ownership to sign Tevez and Javier Mascherano, but the Argentinian forward scored in the last game of the campaign to send Warnock's Blades back down to the Championship.

Warnock was furious, adamant that Tevez shouldn't have been playing. And the court cases that ensued saw West Ham forced to pay £20million in compensation to Sheffield United; yet there was no points deduction and no recompense for Warnock, who lost his job having been relegated with the club he supported as a boy.

The affair still rankles with the manager to this day.

Yet the fact remained, as Warnock approached the 2018/19 campaign with Cardiff, that he had never seen through a full Premier League season without being either relegated or sacked.

There is no doubt events had conspired against him in the past, but the Premier League disappointments with Sheffield United, QPR and his second stint with Crystal Palace – when he was sacked within four months of taking the reins in August 2014 – explain why he was so determined to succeed with Cardiff City.

Recruitment would be key, of course, though Warnock

had learned from his QPR experience and opted against an overhaul of his squad. The bulk of the promotion-winning side were retained on the back of their incredible achievements of the previous season.

While the loan contingent of Craig Bryson, Yanic Wildschut, Liam Feeney, Armand Traore and Jamie Ward all returned to their parent clubs, there were new contracts for an astonishing 11 first-team stars, including Sean Morrison, Joe Ralls, Callum Paterson, Nathaniel Mendez-Laing, Lee Peltier, Neil Etheridge, Bruno Manga, Sol Bamba and Aron Gunnarsson.

"We have been keen to reward the huge effort that the squad put in last season, while it's also fantastic for the club to secure the futures of several key players," said chief executive Ken Choo.

Underperforming big-money signings Lee Tomlin and Gary Madine also remained with the club, but Omar Bogle, Rhys Healey and Stuart O'Keefe were loaned out. Greg Halford's name topped the list of released players.

Halford found it a particularly bitter pill to swallow, having seen the majority of his promotion-winning teammates rewarded with new deals, but he reveals the board had overruled Warnock on this occasion.

"It was a difficult one because I don't think he wanted

me to go, but he was trying to pass it by the board," says Halford.

"I was involved in most of the games that [2017/18] season, but still didn't play many minutes. It was always the last 15, 20 minutes to see out games. I felt like I did that well enough to warrant getting another year.

"I felt like I could have done that in the Premier League, especially with the Premier League experience that I had. But I don't think the board were ever going to allow it, they were looking for someone a bit younger."

Despite the disappointment for Halford, by then aged 33, it was remarkable that so many of the 2017/18 squad stayed together ahead of the new campaign.

* * * *

Stability and future planning. They were the issues on which Warnock and Cardiff could agree. The club craved both financial and footballing solidity, having suffered previously in the Premier League after making too many changes and spending too frivolously under Malky Mackay and Ole Gunnar Solskjaer.

Fans didn't want a repeat of the nightmare that had

become Cardiff's 2013/14 season either, even if the lack of spending risked relegation and tempered excitement. 'In Warnock we trust', was the mantra for many, who appreciated the faith shown in the current crop.

"I think fans bought into Warnock's philosophy and we trusted him to deliver a place in the Premier League again," says supporter Aled Blake.

"That's my personal perspective. You always think 'Could he have made this signing?' but it was right that he backed his own judgement on transfers after the job he'd done.

"Some clubs go up and don't revolutionise their squad, because they understand how important the squad that took them up was. And some clubs do it the other way and spend money. You could probably toss a coin to see which has worked and I think Warnock went with stability because he'd come from nothing with virtually nothing at Cardiff."

Warnock's tactic in the transfer market, then, was to target the best players from the Championship in the hope they could step up and improve. In paying Bristol City £10million for forward Bobby Decordova-Reid, 25, he felt he had identified a player who fit the bill. Josh Murphy, 23, signed from Norwich for £11million, also fell into the same bracket. Warnock also brought in Greg Cunningham and Alex Smithies from Preston and QPR respectively, to bring depth to the left-back and goalkeeping roles.

"He added some quality players from the Championship thinking they're young, they had potential and had proven that in the Championship," adds Blake.

"He didn't get experienced Premier League players, which I think said more about what he was thinking could happen and possible relegation. But I still trusted him to keep us up and I thought he was going to keep us up."

* * * *

The sense of continuity at Cardiff that summer also saw Warnock repeat the previous year's pre-season programme, with another game at Taff's Well before a week touring Devon and Cornwall, where Cardiff beat Tavistock and Bodmin again, before a 1-1 draw at Torquay's Plainmoor. Further pre-season friendlies against Rotherham, Burton Albion and Real Betis were arranged, though it all felt rather low-key.

And while many supporters were satisfied, others couldn't shake the feeling that something needed to be done – that Cardiff were unprepared for a league in which they would face the best in the world. Nathan Blake was among those calling for more holistic changes, in his column and on his podcast.

"It was always a short-term thing," he says on Warnock's plan at Cardiff. "With Neil's team the ball was in the air more than it was on the floor. It was short-term-fix football. You just knew it wasn't going to work in the Premier League even before the end of the promotion season. When Neil stood up outside the castle and said, 'Don't be calling for my head next season', it was because he knew what was coming.

"I said on the *Bootroom* they either needed to change the manager, or get a new assistant coach to help them. They had Neil Warnock's brand of football locked down: playing it long, winning the second ball and playing from there. But Neil had to get help to move forward."

There would be no changes to the coaching staff that summer. Warnock saw things differently.

"I didn't think that the players were capable of changing drastically, because they were used to playing that way," says Warnock.

"He bought one or two, but kept most of the players, so I think it was good man-management to keep it the same," adds Sol Bamba.

And with the squad largely unchanged, he had a squad of players who were happy with his methods. Even the new players were familiar with Cardiff's approach.

Burnley were cited as the model to follow, a medium-sized provincial club who hadn't reinvented the wheel but had built steadily under Sean Dyche to become an established top-flight club. The Clarets, having been promoted in 2015/16, had finished the 2017/18 Premier League campaign in seventh place, playing basic but effective football.

Warnock and Vincent Tan, who gave a rare interview that summer in which he outlined how the club would proceed in the Premier League, were on the same page from both a footballing and financial standpoint.

"We want to follow the Burnley formula and I do think Neil can achieve that with Cardiff," said Tan. "Their methods and what they have managed under Sean Dyche makes football and business sense.

"We are nowhere near other clubs and their billionaire owners who spend so much on players and wages, not even in the Championship.

"We can never be like the two Manchester clubs, or Liverpool, Arsenal, Chelsea or Spurs. We can't be paying silly amounts of money to buy players, we need to be sensible about it. This is sport and it shouldn't just be about throwing big bucks around the whole time. I look at some of the numbers and can't believe them. How can we afford that? We just can't."

And yet it wouldn't have been a Neil Warnock pre-Premier League summer without some late transfer window drama.

A key central midfield signing had eluded the Bluebirds all summer, while there was also a desire to sign another striker given that Decordova-Reid was a number 10 and neither Kenneth Zohore or Madine had fired in pre-season.

They were particularly desperate in midfield, as Aron Gunnarsson was injured again after playing for his country at the 2018 World Cup in Russia and would miss the start of the season. Meanwhile Joe Ralls and Callum Paterson had been overrun by non-league Torquay in midfield a few weeks earlier and looked similarly shaky at Burton, too.

The search went right down to the wire, amid talk of another loan for Liverpool's Marko Grujic, who instead went to Hertha Berlin. Warnock even missed the final minutes of pre-season game at Burton, which ended in a flattering 5-1 win – and subsequent media commitments – because he had to catch a flight to meet a transfer target. It wasn't straightforward, but in the final hours of the window, Cardiff secured loans for Victor Camarasa of Real Betis and Bournemouth's Harry Arter. They didn't get a striker.

The drama hadn't got close to the level of 2011 at QPR, but the fact Cardiff hadn't attracted big-name signings was something of a concern for some fans. On the messageboards and on social media, there were mild grumblings, though nothing major at this stage.

Warnock was just glad it was all over, with Camarasa and Arter genuinely quality additions in his eyes.

"We only got them two right at the death," remembers Warnock. "We didn't spend hardly any money and thank goodness we got them right at the end of the window. They both played their part in the Premier League."

But was it enough? The proof would be in the pudding, though Cardiff's transfer activity had done little to dispel the expectation among pundits and bookmakers that the Bluebirds would struggle.

Chris Sutton stirred the pot with his prediction that the

Bluebirds may even eclipse Derby County as the Premier League's worst ever team. The Rams in 2007/08 earned 11 points and Sutton, on a BBC radio show, said: "When you look at the other sides who have come up, Wolves have spent big money, Fulham have spent big money.

"Cardiff aren't going to score enough goals. They are not good enough to stay in the Premier League. I think Cardiff will go down – maybe with a record low points tally."

After such a modest and understated summer, this was the red rag being flashed into the eyeline of the bull and, on the eve of the new season, it focussed the minds of the Bluebirds' players. Cardiff were already 20th in the bookies' predicted tables and odds-on favourites to go straight back down, but Sutton had stoked the fire.

Warnock had to be realistic speaking at the promotion parade, and while the club pursued a policy of stability in their summer dealings, Cardiff City under his management were a club that just loved to upset the odds. Playing the underdog was second nature to them.

Despite having what most considered to be a Championship standard squad, they believed they could survive and this was another opportunity to prove the doubters wrong.

It would take more than just togetherness, work rate and desire in the Premier League, but they knew in that moment they would throw everything at their bid to survive. Unwittingly, Sutton had done them a favour. They had to look on the bright side. They had to believe.

CHAPTER THIRTEEN

Harsh Reality

It took Cardiff City until the final day of the 2018/19 season to secure a win or draw against one of the Premier League's famed 'big six'. By this point, however, their fate had already been sealed. It was too late.

That amounted to 11 games of the season without a single point accrued, with the majority of the defeats heavy and morale-sapping. A 4-1 reverse at Chelsea, a defeat by the same scoreline at Liverpool, hefty home drubbings by Tottenham and Manchester United, a 5-0 home hammering by Man City; these games, it was agreed, would not determine Cardiff's destiny, yet their nature reflected the chasm Neil Warnock was attempting to bridge throughout the campaign.

Champions Man City, who had just recorded the

Premier League's first 100-point season the previous campaign, formed a mini-league of two alongside Liverpool in 2018/19.

The gap between the top two and third place was 25 points as Pep Guardiola and Jurgen Klopp's sides lost just five games between them all season. Chelsea, Tottenham, Arsenal and Man United jostled for position behind them, all flawed, but still nine points ahead of Wolves who came seventh.

The dominance of the top six clubs throughout the season prompted a number of discussions, both in television studios and living rooms up and down the country, that the league was becoming too slanted in favour of the rich 'superclubs'.

Leicester had shocked the sport in 2015/16 when clinching the league title at 5,000/1 odds, but the big clubs had reacted by flexing their financial muscles. There was little hope for clubs the size of Cardiff, entering this arena for the first time in years. It would be even more improbable for a team to emulate Leicester's heroics and it would be hard enough for the Bluebirds to stay afloat.

Vincent Tan knew this, as did Warnock; that attempting to topple the big boys was impossible, so instead Cardiff concentrated on winning achievable battles. When the

Premier League fixtures were announced in June, the opening months of the campaign offered opportunities for points with matches against Bournemouth, Newcastle, Huddersfield and Burnley in August and September.

Yet even in these eminently winnable games, Cardiff would need to step up their performance level from the one seen in pre-season and in the latter part of their Championship campaign.

Their tactics would need to be refined, as Nathan Blake says: "Why would you sign Victor Camarasa if you're not going to adapt? If you sign Camarasa and Harry Arter, then you have to transition. But if your coaches are doing the same things as before, how are you going to change?"

This was, of course, a regular criticism aimed at Cardiff in the Championship – that their football was outmoded and simplistic – and it became magnified against quality Premier League opposition.

"The quality in the Premier League is so much better, so we did need to adapt a bit," says Sol Bamba. "But I don't think we did anything wrong when it came to the way we approached it."

One of Cardiff's standard tactics was to man-mark each of the opponent's attacking players. In their opening day 2-0 defeat at Bournemouth and later on in the season, it was regularly exposed. The answer for many opposing managers, like the Cherries' Eddie Howe or Tottenham's Mauricio Pochettino, was to have their forward players swap positions, or 'rotate' and thus pull the Bluebirds' defenders out of position.

Bamba recalls the conversation he held with his former Paris Saint-Germain teammate Pochettino about Cardiff's tactics, after a 1-0 defeat to Spurs at Wembley – their temporary home ground that season – in October.

"I do think in the Premier League, though, and the gaffer won't mind me saying this, you can't do man-marking every time," adds Bamba.

"I remember speaking to Pochettino after the Tottenham game and he said, 'We knew, Sol, all we need Harry Kane to do is drag you, Sol, or the captain Morrison, in-field and Dele Alli or [Christian] Eriksen is going to make the run behind you and that's where we're going to create the space. Because we know Cardiff do man-marking'.

"He said, 'Don't get me wrong, because I'd never criticise another manager, especially not one who's been successful', but they knew we were going to play like that."

Bamba relayed the feedback to Warnock, whose response was absolute.

"Sol, why would I change now, after 40 years of being successful in management?"

"He didn't want to change to please everybody and he was right," says Bamba. "I didn't think we got it far wrong. We won a few games and we weren't far away.

"And I don't think Neil should have changed anything. We had success that way and I know the Premier League is the hardest league in the world, but it would have been silly to change too much."

Just like Warnock didn't want to burn his fingers in the transfer market with a series of risky and expensive signings, he believed he had little choice but to stick largely with the tactical methods that his players were accustomed to. Draws against Newcastle and Huddersfield, plus a first win of the campaign – a thumping 4-2 victory over Fulham – gave him the belief that survival was achievable playing this way. And besides, the football was getting a little better slowly but surely.

"I felt in the first few games of the season we still felt like a Championship team in the Premier League," Bamba adds. "But as the season went on everyone started to get more confidence."

Warnock insists that with the help of Kevin Blackwell and Ronnie Jepson on the training field, he was, to a point, honing Cardiff's tactical style for the Premier League. There was some progression from the previous season's 'Warnock Way', if not a complete revolution.

"We got one or two pastings, which I think you do get at that level, but we gave most teams a good work-out," says Warnock.

"I thought we were unlucky at Tottenham when Joe Ralls got sent off and we could quite easily have got a draw there. People say we man-marked a lot but we didn't man-mark as much as what people think – it just looked like that at times.

"We always gave them a little bit more freedom than what people thought. But we had to be disciplined in certain games."

* * * *

Yet it was three away defeats: at Everton, West Ham and Watford during November and December that really dampened pre-season optimism and sowed the seeds of doubt among Cardiff fans. After just one win from their first 11 games, this was more hardship for the fanbase.

The supporters felt these mid-ranking sides could be

beaten, even away from home, and that Warnock lined up his side too defensively. He picked three holding midfielders – Ralls, Arter and Aron Gunnarsson – and played Camarasa out of position on the right flank with Callum Paterson, a former full-back, as his striker. Bobby Decordova-Reid didn't start any of the games. Josh Murphy was in and out of the team.

Despite the scorelines of 1-0 at Everton, 3-1 at West Ham and 3-2 at Watford, in truth Cardiff never came close to winning any of those games.

Fans traipsed back on the buses and trains to South Wales after these grim away days and they slammed Warnock for being over-cautious. Many of the comments and reports in the media were similarly critical.

"We were too respectful of teams," says Aled Blake, who attended many of the games, home and away.

"I don't know whether that was because of what Warnock was telling the players, or if the players were naturally overawed by the whole thing.

"We had a really talented midfielder in Camarasa and some players who could change games, in the likes of Murphy and Decordova-Reid. I suppose the problem was they weren't doing it consistently. I think a lot of people were frustrated by the caution that was shown."

Some of the flak Warnock received was certainly unfair. With regards to his striker selection, he was left with no choice. Kenneth Zohore's form had dropped dramatically from the levels he'd reached in the previous season and a half and with Gary Madine still without a single goal in a Cardiff shirt, the Bluebirds had no selectable striker. Danny Ward scored in the 3-2 defeat to Arsenal, but Warnock wanted height up front and so turned to Paterson – who was far from a recognised centre-forward.

The Scot, to his credit, did an admirable job and scored four goals between 20th October and 8th December. But it was a decision Warnock shouldn't have been forced to make.

Zohore, having previously been rejuvenated by Warnock in dramatic fashion, was a source of major disappointment to his manager, who was adamant he could thrive in the Premier League. Warnock now believes the Dane had become distracted amid the riches of the top flight. The striker would score just one goal all season and left for West Brom in the summer of 2019.

Warnock says: "The problem with Ken was that he did well and we won promotion, and players are so looked-after with agents now.

"I remember Ken coming in with a brand new Bentley

in pre-season and I thought, 'That's wrong'. I didn't think the agent should let him have a car like that and for me he was never the same."

But many points raised by the fans in this period were valid. They were right in wanting to see more of the exciting Camarasa, who had caught the eye from his debut appearance against Newcastle and scored a fine goal against Arsenal. In the Spaniard, there was hope of a more free-flowing style and some dangerous attacking football. He was wasted on the right wing, while Decordova-Reid was being wasted completely.

Despite the murmurings of discontent and the fact Cardiff were firmly embedded in the bottom three until November, in general the Bluebirds fans remained firmly behind their manager.

That togetherness, which had been harnessed from the previous campaign, extending from the dressing room to the terraces – and reinforced by the viral hashtag #CityAsOne – was keeping the club united. So while Fulham sacked Slavisa Jokanovic and Southampton gave Mark Hughes his marching orders amid discontent from their fans, there were no such fears for Warnock. He was still the kingpin.

The Cardiff boss felt he could be more gung-ho in

his team selections on home turf, often dropping Ralls to accommodate Camarasa in a more central area and playing a genuine winger on the right in his 4-5-1, which could become a 4-2-3-1 when attacking.

This was the way the Bluebirds played in three successive home victories, against Brighton, Wolves and Southampton – teams in that mid-table bracket Cardiff had targeted. Despite some of the turgid football on the road, Cardiff City Stadium was becoming a fortress again.

That run of consecutive home wins came crashing to an end in strange circumstances, however, as Ole Gunnar Solskjaer – newly appointed as Manchester United manager, replacing Jose Mourinho in December – returned to the Welsh capital to exact some form of revenge for his ill-fated Bluebirds spell.

United romped to a 5-1 win in Solskjaer's debut match, with Warnock furious at his side's defending, even against world-class stars like Marcus Rashford, Paul Pogba and Anthony Martial.

But such was Cardiff's home form in the previous weeks, they remained in 17th, out of the drop zone, on Christmas Day. A Boxing Day 0-0 draw at Crystal Palace cemented this position at the season's halfway mark.

Fifteen points from 19 games, with Burnley, Fulham

and Huddersfield all below Neil Warnock's side. A solid start to life in the top flight? Cardiff certainly felt so, despite the numerous on-field issues that Warnock had encountered following promotion.

But their away form and a lack of attacking edge remained problematic. It was time to kick on.

CHAPTER FOURTEEN

The Victor

Leicester 0-1 Cardiff, 29th December 2018
Leicester: (4-2-3-1): Schmeichel; Pereira, Soyuncu, Maguire, Chilwell; Mendy, Ndidi; Albrighton (Ghezzal, 58), Maddison, Gray (Okazaki, 79); Vardy (Iheanacho, 68).
Subs not used: Ward, Fuchs, Simpson, Iborra.
Cardiff (4-3-3): Etheridge; Manga, Morrison, Bamba, Cunningham; Gunnarsson, Arter (Peltier, 90+5), Camarasa; Hoilett (Decordova-Reid, 83), Murphy (Harris, 78) Paterson.
Subs not used: Smithies, Bennett, Rals, Mendez-Laing.
Cardiff goal: Camarasa (90+2).

The adaptation period for teams entering the Premier League can vary from club to club. Some, like Ipswich in

2000/01 and Reading in 2006/07, can take the division by storm from the very first game and finish in the top half, though in both cases their rapid rise tailed off just as quickly as they had benefited from being an unknown quantity. Teams soon worked them out.

Others can develop more gradually and settle on a method that guarantees survival for a longer period of time, like Southampton from 2012 and Leicester City from 2014. The aim for Cardiff City, like all those had gone before them, was to establish themselves as a Premier League force.

In every case, a team needs a lightbulb moment, a game in which they truly feel like a Premier League side. By Sol Bamba's own admission, Cardiff spent the opening few games of the 2018/19 campaign trying to convince themselves they belonged in English football's top tier.

Pundits like the aforementioned Chris Sutton, who treated them with a dismissive attitude, didn't help.

Neither did their atrocious away form, which in itself was becoming a stick with which to beat the Bluebirds. But after the draw at Crystal Palace on Boxing Day – and their first away clean sheet – Neil Warnock's men headed to Leicester's King Power Stadium on 29th December feeling quietly confident of securing more precious points in their bid for survival. They would have to beat a team who themselves had just toppled some of the league's frontrunners, with Claude Puel's side having stunned Manchester City and Chelsea in their previous two outings. The Foxes sat seventh before their meeting with Cardiff; they were the best of the rest.

Puel paid Cardiff their dues, picking a strong side that included Premier League winners Kasper Schmeichel, Marc Albrighton and Jamie Vardy. Also starting was England's World Cup centre-back Harry Maguire and irresistible playmaker James Maddison, formerly of Norwich, and already known to Cardiff from the previous season in the Championship.

Having picked a back five at Selhurst Park three days earlier, Warnock reverted to his 4-5-1 (or 4-3-3 depending on your viewpoint) in a slightly more attacking line-up, with Victor Camarasa in his favoured central slot and Josh Murphy and Junior Hoilett out wide. Callum Paterson remained the best striking option.

The only surprise was to see Greg Cunningham at left-back instead of Joe Bennett. And the former Preston full-back was clearly a little nervous on just his sixth league start for the Bluebirds since his £3million summer transfer, misjudging a backpass to Neil Etheridge in the opening five minutes that rolled inches wide of his own post. Almost a nightmare start.

Otherwise, Cardiff started well, sensing Leicester were a little apprehensive and, with the help of a vocal travelling contingent from the Welsh capital, were again thriving in their preferred underdog role.

Vardy had, by this stage in his career, gained a reputation as the Foxes' talisman and a favourite with the King Power crowd, though he barely got a kick in the first half thanks to the defensive shackling of Bamba and Sean Morrison. And for once, the Cardiff midfield was looking mobile and cohesive, keeping the ball for long stretches and probing for openings – thanks largely to Camarasa.

The Spaniard was a special player, and the story of how his loan move to Cardiff had come about was intriguing.

Cardiff scouts were present at a pre-season friendly between Real Betis and Bournemouth – ahead of the Bluebirds' Premier League season opener against the south coast side – when they stumbled across Camarasa. Word on the street was that this eye-catching midfield roamer could be available for a loan.

The 24-year-old realised himself that he wasn't in manager Quique Setien's first-team plans for the coming season at Betis.

His girlfriend Carla Vila ended up playing a huge part in the decision to swap Seville for South Wales in August 2018. She had lived in the city before and hugely enjoyed it, so persuaded Camarasa to step into the unknown. Warnock could scarcely believe Betis had been happy to let such a talent leave on loan.

"We need somebody like Victor's missus, don't we, who's been to Cardiff and has loved Cardiff, to talk him into coming. I keep thanking his missus," Warnock joked when talking about future signings from abroad, a market he would explore further after the successful acquisition of Camarasa.

The midfielder was also a fine example of how Warnock could work with creative players after all, amid criticism of the way he had handled Camarasa's playmaking predecessor at Cardiff, Lee Tomlin, and current forward Bobby Decordova-Reid.

In signing Tomlin from Bristol City in summer 2017 the Cardiff boss thought he had found the next iteration of QPR'S 2010/2011 magic man, Adel Taarabt, the one-in-a-million talent who had loved playing under Warnock. Decorvoda-Reid was another one, a number 10 who was being underused by Warnock in the eyes of many supporters, but whose initial arrival at Cardiff made supporters expectant and excited about a more fluent style. Neither Tomlin nor Decordova-Reid lacked footballing ability but they didn't fire under Warnock for a multitude of reasons.

"Some players and managers just don't fit together," says Glen Williams of *WalesOnline*.

"Tomlin and Decordova-Reid are both flair players who go against the grain a bit and produce moments of magic, but they don't necessarily fit into a rigid system that Warnock likes."

"The players that you would have thought would be more conducive to Premier League football like your Tomlins, Decordova-Reid – they hardly featured," adds Nathan Blake.

"I understood it from Neil's perspective. He stuck with what he knew, what had got him seven promotions... So why change things at the age of 70?"

Camarasa was undoubtedly a flair player too, but Warnock had managed to harness the skill of the on-loan Real Betis man and channel it within a structured framework.

"I loved Victor, he was another one who needed someone like me," says Warnock. "He was another Taarabt, but a little bit more disciplined. But he had that magic about him and he needed someone to believe in him. He was a good foil for us."

Warnock would never manage that with Tomlin, who had come back to Cardiff after spending the second half of the 2017/18 season on loan at Nottingham Forest, but wasn't training with the first-team squad.

Warnock had become hugely frustrated with him, having offered him a final shot at retribution on the eve of the Premier League campaign, so long as the player could find fitness and consistent form. It didn't happen. Ultimately, Tomlin could never be Warnock's Taarabt mark two.

And while Decordova-Reid still had time to prove his worth, Camarasa was proving to be the real deal. Some believed the Premier League's quicker tempo and the tactical demands of Warnock's system at Cardiff would be too much for him. The Leicester game was a reflection of how wrong they were.

So although Leicester got better as the first half unfolded, on a cold afternoon just after Christmas, Cardiff held firm. Etheridge made a solid save from Maddison midway through the opening 45 minutes, before bravely smothering the ball away from Vardy after a fine through ball. Maddison was new to the Premier League, fresh out of the Championship like Cardiff, but the Bluebirds were struggling to constrain him. He was the orchestra conductor, on a level that surpassed what even Camarasa was capable of.

But Warnock's coaching staff looked to have devised an effective strategy, with Paterson dropping deep as the target man and laying the ball off to Murphy, Hoilett and Camarasa – the runners from midfield. Defensive shuttlers Harry Arter and Aron Gunnarsson focussed on suppressing Maddison.

On 66 minutes, Murphy came close to the opener, but Schmeichel parried away his left-footed effort. Paterson had earlier spurned a couple of decent chances.

The Bluebirds' performance level was much higher than in previous away games, but the sucker punch came after 73 minutes when Morrison tugged on Maddison's shirt and referee Simon Hooper pointed for a penalty.

Warnock's face said it all.

His exasperation was clear as he turned away – he never watches penalties live – expecting the dreaded roar of the home crowd to celebrate a Maddison goal from the spot. Vardy, Leicester's usual penalty-taker, had been substituted so the young number 10 stepped up instead.

Then something happened. Divine intervention?

Maybe. A sensational Etheridge penalty save followed by a despairing Bamba tackle as Maddison was denied twice. The home fans fell into shocked silence and the away fans erupted. Cardiff were, deservedly, still on level terms.

Warnock could breathe again. Was this Cardiff's moment?

Throughout the game, Camarasa had continued to pick up the ball 30 or 35 yards from the Leicester goal. Each time, he'd either had a pot shot, or laid the ball out wide.

Warnock had a word at half-time, issuing one of his famous pep talks. He knew what he wanted from his creative catalyst after the break.

"Keep shooting – I'll never shout at you," were the words of wisdom, Warnock revealed after the game.

Aided by the fresh legs of Kadeem Harris and Decordova-Reid off the substitutes' bench, Cardiff retained an attacking threat until the last minute. The 92nd minute, to be precise, when Arter won the ball deep in Leicester territory and found Decordova-Reid on the edge of the box. His layoff was taken perfectly in the stride of Camarasa, who thundered the ball into the top corner from more than 30 yards.

The Cardiff players, coaching staff and fans around the ground could not contain themselves. The sense of achievement and relief was palpable in the bedlam that followed, Camarasa whipping off his shirt and screaming 'Vamos!' – come on – over and over.

They had finally done it – and might actually have won 2-0 as Harris came close before the full-time whistle.

As the celebrations continued after the game, you had to remind yourself this was just three points. The battle to stave off relegation was only half done, and yet it felt like a potential turning point in the Bluebirds' season.

"We've had opportunities this season – we've missed penalties and everything else away from home. This was the first time away from home that we've deserved to win," Warnock admitted to Leicester legend Gary Lineker on BBC's *Match of the Day* that night. "We were the better team if I'm being honest."

Not for the first time, he'd summed it up perfectly. Etheridge was named man of the match, Bamba was a colossus in defence, but the plaudits belonged to the incredible Camarasa, who was quickly declared a cult hero by the supporters. They sang his name all night.

Cardiff had their away win, their lightbulb moment. The table made for enjoyable reading for fans, too, with Warnock's side sitting 16th on 18 points, four above the drop zone. From a footballing perspective, the tide was turning in the Bluebirds' favour. This was a brilliantly victorious night, though as Warnock knew better than most, you can never savour the wins for too long.

CHAPTER FIFTEEN

Tragedy

And so 2019 arrived, with Cardiff City feeling the optimism that always comes with the start of a new year. They were boosted by the Leicester result and the opening of the transfer window, which would finally give Neil Warnock an opportunity to make those much-needed repairs to his squad. Top of his transfer wish list was a striker; and in an ideal world he would sign a right-back and a central midfielder too.

Not even a New Year's Day defeat at home to Tottenham Hotspur could puncture the mood around Cardiff City Stadium, though two more underwhelming results would focus minds on the transfer search. A disappointing surprise FA Cup exit at Gillingham, where a second-string Cardiff side lost 1-0, and a frustrating goalless home draw to Huddersfield – in which Warnock's side had dominated but lacked a clinical touch – left Cardiff fans feeling anxious for new arrivals.

Finding someone to supply the goals, it was universally agreed, would surely fire the Bluebirds to safety and was marked top priority by the club's transfer committee. Warnock settled on a transfer list that saw Liverpool's Nathaniel Clyne, OGC Nice midfielder Adrien Tameze and Nantes striker Emiliano Sala emerge as priority targets. If they could secure those three signings, Cardiff's chances of cementing their Premier League status looked very good indeed.

But something else – something unprecedented and quite frankly unimaginable – was about to happen. It would make the Leicester win, the battle to avoid relegation and football in its entirety, pale into insignificance.

* * * *

The fateful flight that Emiliano Sala took from Nantes to Cardiff, on the evening of Monday 21st January 2019, should have been the start of a new chapter. It ought to have brought an end to weeks of uncertainty for Neil

TRAGEDY

Warnock, Sala and Cardiff City, as the club's record signing prepared to touch down in his new home, to play for his new team.

Supporters could not wait to see him in action after his signing was announced on the Saturday 19th January. Sala had been in Cardiff to confirm his arrival on the Friday, with a picture then posted on social media 24 hours later showing him holding up a Bluebirds shirt. He had been taken around Cardiff City Stadium to meet club officials but headed back to Nantes to gather his belongings.

Sala, too, was hugely excited if a little apprehensive about making the transfer. He had initially needed convincing that it was the right move but was glad to be a Cardiff player.

"I'm very happy to be here," Sala told the club's media team. "It gives me great pleasure and I can't wait to start training, meet my new teammates and get down to work. For me it feels special.

"I have come here wanting to work and to help my teammates and the club. I can't wait to get to work straight away and do everything I can."

The events that followed are now infamous throughout the world as one of the most shocking tragedies in the history of professional football unfolded, with Cardiff City at the epicentre.

The Piper Malibu light aircraft that was carrying Sala crashed into the English Channel on the night of 21st January, with the 28-year-old Argentinian later found dead. The body of the pilot, David Ibbotson, has never been discovered.

The fall-out from Sala's death continues to this day and has been complex and unpleasant in equal measure. It has included a police inquiry into manslaughter, an ongoing aviation investigation into the crash itself plus a Court of Arbitration for Sport dispute about the £15million transfer fee Cardiff were due to pay Nantes.

Initial complications concerning agents, the pilot's suitability for flying and the true owners of the aircraft made the entire affair all the more tragic and unpalatable. But for Warnock and Cardiff fans the feeling was clear and overwhelming: utter devastation, heartbreak.

Sala had been a Cardiff transfer target for a number of weeks, after Warnock had initially watched videos of him and quickly came to the conclusion that this was his type of player.

The Cardiff boss became a genuine admirer of Sala as a footballer and later as a character. Warnock had convinced Mehmet Dalman and the Cardiff transfer committee to part with a club-record £15million for the striker. The manager later revealed his reasons for the prolonged transfer interest in a press conference after the player's disappearance.

"I said to him, he's what I call an ugly footballer, a scruffy footballer," he said. "I said that is why he will go down well with us. He gave everything, 100 per cent, every time he played.

"He didn't always play well, but he scored some great goals and I think he was just so looking forward to the challenge of coming here."

Warnock twice watched the Argentinian play in person amid his search for a goalscorer to help Cardiff avoid relegation. The 6ft 2inch target man was at the peak of his powers; only Paris Saint-Germain superstar Kylian Mbappe had scored more goals in the French Ligue 1 than Sala by that stage of the season. Along with Cardiff's January loan signing Oumar Niasse from Everton, he was tipped to supply the goals to keep them up.

Warnock and his assistant Kevin Blackwell flew to Nantes on 5th December, the day after Cardiff's 3-1 defeat at West Ham's London Stadium, to watch Sala close up for the first time.

Also on board were noted agent Willie McKay – with whom Warnock had worked in the past – and his son Mark, who organised and paid for the flight.

On 6th January, Warnock took the club's player liaison officer Callum Davies with him on a second flight from Cardiff to Nantes to meet Sala in person and watch the player in action against Montpellier.

Sala impressed on both occasions, scoring in the first game against Marseille but playing "much better" in the second outing, in Warnock's words. Both journeys made by the Cardiff manager were on aircraft chartered by the McKays, with Warnock later admitting that he had travelled on similar planes to the one that had crashed with Sala on board.

Willie McKay was not a registered agent at the time, but helped his son act as an official intermediary on a mandate from Nantes to sell players, with the French club's chairman Waldemar Kita eager to sell Sala amid the Premier League interest. Even a club like Cardiff, with the smallest budget in the top flight in the 2018/19 season, would pay a huge fee relative to Nantes' own finances. Kita felt January was the time to sell and enlisted the help of the McKays.

A letter sent by Willie McKay to Sala later emerged

revealing the agent had suggested Sala could one day play for Manchester United, Chelsea or Liverpool. He also informed the player that there was apparent interest from West Ham, Everton and Leicester, among others, though the only obvious bidders were Cardiff.

At one stage it had looked like the transfer might not happen, despite the fact it seemed to work well for all parties. As well as Nantes, Mark McKay and Sala's own personal representative – French agent Meissa N'Diaye – would get a cut of the deal, while Warnock's Bluebirds would get the influx of goals their season so badly needed.

For a while, Sala was uncertain about the move and whether he would shine in the Premier League, having had a modest career at Caen and Bordeaux before joining Nantes. He also wasn't sure that Cardiff were the right team. Although he idolised Argentine legend Gabriel Batistuta, who had played for some of Europe's biggest clubs, Sala felt settled in Nantes. That was the reason he had rejected a move to Turkish side Galatasaray the previous summer.

But Sala was also ambitious, having moved to Europe from his native Santa Fe as a teenager to pursue his dream. And he knew he was in the best form of his life. Playing in the Premier League was still a huge lure for him.

So after a few weeks of tos and fros and conversations between Warnock and Sala, the most expensive deal in Cardiff City's history was announced on the evening of Saturday 19th January, just hours after they had been thrashed 3-0 at Newcastle.

Given the Bluebirds' slump since beating Leicester, the arrival of Sala was highly anticipated.

Warnock now reveals he had wanted the player to join his squad at St James' Park – as a spectator, since he wasn't yet registered with the Premier League – instead of going back home to Nantes that weekend. It's a conversation that still haunts him.

"Having met him, you do ask questions of yourself," says Warnock, looking back. "I remember going over to him on the training ground on the Friday and saying, 'Do you want to come with us to Newcastle?'

"I often think, 'Why didn't I make him come with us?' Why didn't I insist?

"He wanted to get all his gear and say goodbye to the lads over there. And then something like that happens – you can't legislate for something like that."

Nantes held a special place in Sala's heart after his three-and-a-half seasons with the French club. And having agonised over whether to agree to the Cardiff transfer before signing a contract worth around £50,000 per week, Sala wanted to say farewell properly. He posted a picture on his Instagram account on Monday lunchtime showing him arm-in-arm with his former teammates and the caption "La ultima ciao" – the final goodbye.

When the news came through that Sala hadn't reached Cardiff on the Monday night, that image became horribly prophetic. And for Warnock and the Cardiff players, having met the 28-year-old and spoken about the impact he might have up front, the whole experience was harrowing.

Sol Bamba, along with Callum Davies, had been involved in some of the negotiations with Sala as an interpreter, being a native French speaker. He reveals the immediate impressions Sala made on that Friday in Cardiff and how excited the squad were about their new addition.

"It made it worse that he'd actually met a few of the lads", says Bamba. "Everyone was looking forward to seeing him coming back and helping us stay in the Premier League.

"It affected every single one of us, the gaffer in particular. He said to me he shouldn't have let him go, he thought he should have asked Emiliano to stay in the UK. I was doing the translation and he asked me to say to Emiliano to come and watch the game against Newcastle and from there go and fly home to get his stuff.

"There was nothing anyone could have done. I remember being with Neil in his office in floods of tears thinking about it."

* * * *

What made matters even worse for everyone involved was the long wait for answers from the moment the news broke on Tuesday morning.

First there was the revelation that an aircraft, carrying two unknown passengers, bound for Cardiff Airport coming from Nantes had gone missing. It was reported that the pilot had first requested to descend sharply amid poor visibility in the January wind and rain but lost contact with Jersey air traffic control soon after.

The plane was then declared missing somewhere north of Guernsey in the Channel Islands some time after 8pm. The initial night-time search was called off at 2am.

The first sign that something might be wrong came from Callum Davies, who had messaged Sala and was waiting for him to land at Cardiff Airport. Davies reported to club bosses that the aircraft was nowhere to be seen, striking them with fear and worry.

They cancelled Tuesday's training session – the first one Sala had been due to attend – and Dalman released a statement admitting everyone at the club was "very concerned for the safety of Emiliano Sala".

Soon after their worst fears were realised; it was confirmed Sala was on board the plane, along with pilot David Ibbotson.

There followed the French authorities' official search and rescue effort, with assistance from the British Coastguard, though after no progress was made, it was abandoned on Thursday 24th January. Both Sala and Mr Ibbotson remained missing, but both were presumed to be dead.

Meanwhile, questions emerged about who had booked the plane, Mr Ibbotson's pilot's credentials were investigated and it was claimed by Bluebirds officials that Sala's transfer registration hadn't been fully completed. The mood around the cities of Cardiff and Nantes was of utter confusion. Despair.

Where Cardiff City went from here was anyone's guess. Fortunately they had no fixture to fulfil that weekend as they were no longer in the FA Cup, so players and coaching staff were given time off and offered counselling as everyone tried to come to terms with the unthinkable. On that Saturday, Warnock switched off his phone and escaped to a hotel in Narbeth, in Pembrokeshire, with wife Sharon. He didn't know how to react.

The wider footballing world responded in emotional and spirited style. Sala's fellow Argetinians, world superstars Lionel Messi and Sergio Aguero, were among those to demand the search was continued. Sala's family had led the calls, and £259,000 was raised via an online charity page. The search was resumed by private 'shipwreck hunter' David Mearns.

Thousands of flowers, flags and shirts began to appear outside Cardiff City Stadium's Fred Keenor statue and remained there for weeks afterwards, while Nantes fans also paid tribute to their fallen comrade with a stunning tifo display before their home clash with Saint-Etienne.

For the Bluebirds, the feeling was equally as strange as it was upsetting.

Cardiff fans had never seen Sala in action. Some of the players and staff had never met him. Yet he truly felt like a part of their club, because he'd agreed to join their cause, and his disappearance and subsequent death was bringing everyone even closer together.

Warnock was again at the heart of that process. A unifying figure, as he'd been in the past, although he had found these circumstances especially tough.

Asked in his first press conference after the tragedy if he'd considered walking away from football altogether, Warnock said: "I think probably 24 hours a day in the last week, yeah.

"Because there's more important things, aren't there? It takes something like that to make you realise. But I [also] realise I have a job to do here, and it was always a massive job.

"It's doubly massive now, and that's when you've got to show your leadership and show the lads you're in charge of that we've got another miracle to do here. Another obstacle and we just have to move on and try and prove this miracle."

Looking back, Warnock stands by those words.

"I did feel 'was it worth it?' Football is only a game," he says. "It's how I felt when Sharon had breast cancer. But I did feel more responsible if anything, that I had to get us through this, the players, the board, Mehmet, the fans and everyone.

"I felt responsibility [to ensure] that we came through the other side."

Although their footballing preparations had been hit by the tragedy, Cardiff still had to prepare for a game against Arsenal on Tuesday 29th January. Sala – who was still missing at the time – was named on the official team sheet; a poignant gesture from the Gunners. A minute's silence was observed and the away fans held up yellow placards, the colours of Nantes.

"We were superb that night," remembers Warnock, with Cardiff unlucky to lose 2-1 at the Emirates.

Three days later they were convincing winners over Bournemouth in a 2-0 victory at an emotional Cardiff City Stadium, Bobby Decordova-Reid getting both goals.

As they had done at Arsenal, the Cardiff fans paid tribute to Sala by wearing yellow daffodils and aired their new song: "Sing a song for Sala. We will never let you go. You will always be at the City here with me."

It reverberated around the stadium long after the final whistle had sounded, with tears streaming down Warnock's face as he clapped all four sides of the ground. This was more than just a win. This was for Emiliano. For Emi.

"It was another unifying event in the club's history," remembers Aled Blake, who attended the Bournemouth game that day in the Welsh capital. "And one that further knitted together that disparate fanbase that had been so talked about in the previous seasons. We did rally and it was an emotional time."

"The Bournemouth game at home – wow," says Warnock. "I think we'd have beaten anybody that day. In the dressing room beforehand it was how to calm us down a bit. They were ready to take on anybody."

Bamba was magnificent in both the Arsenal and Bournemouth games but admitted he was fighting to keep control of his emotions.

"It was huge. Forget about football, forget about everything else, it was just a big tragedy," he says. "Losing someone like that, you think about his mum and dad, his family and friends. None of the players had ever experienced anything like that.

"It's difficult to talk about it and everyone dealt with it the best way they could. Looking back, I don't think you can ever deal with it the right way."

The Sala family: his sister Romina, mother Mercedes and father Horacio, as well as Cardiff City and Nantes, eventually got closure on 7th February, more than two weeks after the disappearance, when a body was found and identified as Emiliano Sala.

Football had already been in mourning for some time,

though with that announcement the final hope of some good news was extinguished.

* * * *

The actions of the club in the weeks after the tragedy had been highly commended by the media, despite the various legal wrangles that were to come.

Yet the next part would be equally difficult given the sensitive circumstances. How could Cardiff complete any further January transfer deals when they were still reeling from a truly traumatic event?

While Niasse – the only January signing before Sala – had started well enough up front, from a purely footballing point of view, Cardiff needed more reinforcements to "prove the miracle" of staying in the league, as Warnock put it. And while Sala's disappearance and death had put football into perspective, their manager felt they had a new cause to fight for.

But how much did football really matter to him? The idea of Neil Warnock considering the game unimportant would even a few weeks ago have felt ludicrous. But nothing would ever be the same again. Not even 40 years of managerial experience could help Warnock now. "With the Emiliano tragedy, you can't really cater for anything like that," he says.

"I thought he would be the answer, because we just needed someone who could put it in the net but worked hard. He was our kind of player."

Cardiff had back-up striking options on their list, in case they couldn't sign Sala, and the final few days of the January window would see Warnock and Dalman try to clinch a last-gasp deal, while Ken Choo dutifully and dignifiedly kept the club running in the wake of the tragedy. Choo along with Warnock, Davies and club media manager Mark Denham would later attend Sala's funeral in Santa Fe, too.

On the transfer front, Warnock had already been stung by Liverpool in his pursuit of a loan deal for Nathaniel Clyne. This was one he wanted to wrap up early in the window to solve an issue at right-back, where Bruno Manga had been playing out of position. Warnock later learned via his television that Clyne was going to Bournemouth instead, accusing Liverpool of "lacking class" after they failed to call him.

Monaco's Almamy Toure and Marseille full-back Bouna Sarr were identified as Clyne replacements but with finances in a tricky position given the Sala situation, no deal could be done.

And while Dalman tried to revive a deal for midfielder Adrien Tameze later in the window, flying to Nice to negotiate a deal, neither the player nor his manager Patrick Vieira were keen on a sale.

Cardiff found it tricky to shore up the midfield in the wake of the Sala tragedy, since it was difficult to give any kind of transfer their full attention.

The final two days of the window then saw Warnock consider and contact a number of strikers, still optimistic of a deal that would bring hope of a successful battle against relegation. Wesley Moraes and Mbwana Samatta, who both later joined Aston Villa, were targeted, as was Sebastien Haller, latterly of West Ham. Bayer Leverkusen's Lucas Alario was another target, while Charlie Austin and Vincent Janssen were briefly considered.

The chilling truth, as Warnock says, is that the strikers didn't want to come to Cardiff for fear of being considered Sala's replacement. The time wasn't right.

"You can understand why they didn't want to come," says Warnock. "They thought it was like tempting fate. One of the lads said, 'I'm sorry Neil, I don't really want to be the one that takes his place,' and I'd never thought about it like that, to be honest. But it was hard work, mentally and physically for me."

In the end, after a frantic deadline day, Cardiff were only able to announce one deal, a £3million move for Reading's Leandro Bacuna. It was another signing from the Championship but it was at least an extra pair of legs and someone who could play at right-back or in midfield.

Ultimately, and completely understandably, the Sala affair had taken its toll and the thought of putting so much work into a transfer suddenly felt futile.

"The season became secondary to the fact a player had died," says Blake. "And that overtook anything else. Perspective-wise the death of a player outweighed everything."

It would become a running theme for the rest of Cardiff's season. Everything they did was inextricably linked to Emiliano Sala, for better or worse.

Whether they were relegated or not, Neil Warnock and his team felt they were playing for Emi.

CHAPTER SIXTEEN

Fight Until The End

After the storm, came the battle. But between the two was a question that everyone connected to Cardiff City was asking themselves in the aftermath of the Emiliano Sala tragedy: did they really care about staying in the Premier League anymore? As one supporter told journalists outside Cardiff City Stadium following Sala's death: "We'd rather have got relegated with him than stay up without him." It was aptly put.

Yet behind the scenes Neil Warnock was engineering a renewed sense of quiet defiance in his Cardiff players. If they could have turned back time, they would. But the only thing left to do was what Warnock and his Bluebirds knew best: scrap for every point.

It was time to grit their teeth and win the hearts of

the wider footballing public with a series of spirited displays. It started at Southampton, Cardiff's first match since Sala's body was found and his death confirmed, an opportunity for closure.

The players warmed up in blue T-shirts adorned with Sala's image and the 3,000 away fans' noise had built steadily up until kick-off. St Mary's Stadium, which – way back in April 2014 – had been the location of Cardiff's only previous Premier League away win before the Leicester victory, appeared to offer the Bluebirds another great chance of points.

It turned out to be a famous afternoon, not just because the Sala tributes continued, but because of arguably the most characterful display of Cardiff's season.

The game saw Cardiff finally score from a set-piece – one of their strengths in the Championship but strangely impotent to this point in the top flight – after Sol Bamba broke the deadlock on 69 minutes. Callum Paterson's knock-down dropped perfectly for the defender to slot home before racing head-first into the mass of Cardiff fans behind the goal.

One supporter, 18-year-old Noah Bushby, smashed his glasses while celebrating with Bamba. Neither of them particularly cared in the moment, but Bamba being the gentleman later contacted him on Twitter, saying: "Sorry for your glasses, big man. You hugged me harder than my wife ever did" – and then helped Noah pay for a replacement pair.

The away fans at Southampton thought the celebrations had all been for nothing, however, when Saints' Jack Stephens broke Cardiff hearts with a 91st-minute equaliser. A draw, although creditable, would have felt like a defeat as the Stephens strike punctured the spirit and defiant mood among the Cardiff supporters.

Not for long, though, as substitute Kenneth Zohore – thrown on hopefully by Warnock to play in a double-pronged attack with Oumar Niasse – snatched a 93rd-minute winner in dramatic fashion. Cardiff frantically kept the ball alive in one last, desperate, attack with Victor Camarasa's trademark composure playing a huge part, laying the ball back for Zohore to drill in the bottom corner.

More chaotic celebrations in the Cardiff end, with Zohore ripping off his shirt and screaming "I'm back!" He hadn't scored a goal for 10 months.

But it certainly felt like Cardiff were indeed back, having now secured consecutive wins in the Premier League for the first time in the season and leapfrogging

Southampton with that precious victory, which put them 16th on 25 points, one above the relegation zone.

An emotional Warnock again declared the win to be a fitting tribute to Sala. "It's been difficult for everybody," he told the media afterwards. "We wanted to do it for Emiliano and I'm really proud that the lads have done him justice."

* * * *

The Southampton win somehow felt like it marked the end of the most difficult period in Cardiff City's history. But, despite an international break meaning Cardiff didn't have a fixture the next weekend, there would never be enough time to properly reflect on the events of January 2019.

The relentlessness of the Premier League soon bit again and provided the true footballing test for Warnock's side. And although two previously underused forwards, in Bobby Decordova-Reid and Zohore, had helped secure the wins over Bournemouth and Southampton respectively, there was still time for Cardiff's season to take another two or three twists.

Supporter Aled Blake remembers: "We won that Southampton game and you did think after that, 'Ooh maybe we can do it', because our away form had been so abysmal before that.

"But our next game was at home to Watford and they hammered us. We couldn't deal with Gerard Deulofeu."

There followed three deflating but ultimately deserved defeats for Cardiff, the first one coming 5-1 at home to a Deulofeu-inspired Watford, before a 3-0 home reverse to Everton and then a meek – and out of character – performance to lose 2-0 at Wolves. The spirit that seemed to be coursing through the veins of the Cardiff players against Arsenal, Bournemouth and Southampton was nowhere to be seen anymore.

"I think long-term the Sala tragedy really did negatively affect the club," adds Blake. "I get that Warnock wanted to finish the job and perform his duties as manager, but it was really tough for him. Had that not happened, not only would someone not have lost their life but maybe our season would have been different."

Yet Warnock was keen that Cardiff did not use the tragic circumstances as an excuse. He knew his side's chances of staying in the league were slim beforehand and that this event had made his job doubly difficult.

Another blow had arrived during the defeat at Molineux as Bamba was taken off on a stretcher with what appeared to be a serious injury. He had captained the team in the absence of the injured Sean Morrison for most of January and February and scored big goals against Chelsea, Brighton, Southampton and Watford. It was another slice of bad luck for Cardiff.

It was soon confirmed that Bamba had ruptured his knee ligaments in the Wolves game and would need surgery. Having played such a crucial part in the entire Warnock tenure, one of the main men would not be there to see through the fight against relegation.

"For me from a personal point of view it was even more disappointing because I couldn't help the team," says Bamba. "I chatted to the lads after I got injured and I felt that I was letting them down – and the players were almost fighting me saying, 'You can't say that!'.

"I was in Barcelona for the surgery and I flew in to support the lads to watch the final few games, against the medical staff's advice, to try and make sure we were all there together."

Despite the loss of Bamba and the three defeats, Cardiff remained in the mix to stay up. Huddersfield and Fulham were adrift below them, but the battle to avoid relegation looked to include several other sides in the group above the Bluebirds: Newcastle, Burnley, Brighton and Southampton.

A 2-1 home victory for Cardiff against West Ham on 9th March kept them in the hunt, but the microscope was beginning to turn – from some fans – onto Warnock himself. The argument that his tactics weren't up to the task reared its head again in some circles, although there was still a majority who backed Warnock to the hilt and wouldn't countenance the criticism.

While the Wolves loss swung the argument one way, the West Ham win brought some of the doubters back onside. It was a constant pendulum.

"I had this debate all through the Premier League season with family and friends about him being in charge and whether it was a season too far," says Aled Blake on Warnock's role.

"I think the odds were stacked against us from the start, because that squad was probably never good enough."

By this stage, Warnock had shut out the noise. He'd stuck to his guns and felt compelled to keep in place his old methods, as he maintains to this day: "We had a way and by the end I thought we could finish above Southampton, Brighton and Burnley."

And as well as his personal ambition to finally succeed in the Premier League, and Cardiff's chequered history in it, he wanted to do it for Sala.

So after the West Ham game, three of the Bluebirds' next four fixtures would determine their fate. Chelsea at home, Burnley away, Brighton away.

You could not have written a script of what happened during Cardiff 1-2 Chelsea on 31st March for fear of it seeming too far-fetched.

Warnock's men had proven more than competitive in an even first half and saw appeals for a penalty – when Marcos Alonso pulled on Morrison's shirt – waved away by referee Craig Pawson. That would be just the first on the list of Cardiff's frustrations that afternoon.

Despite going ahead through a delicious Camarasa volley within a minute of the restart, and the fact Chelsea's supporters were infuriated with their side's own slow passing play under manager Maurizio Sarri, the game would turn on its head in the final 10 minutes. Cesar Azpilicueta equalised in the 84th minute for Chelsea with a header, though was shown on the replays to be yards offside when he put the ball into the net.

And although there was nothing wrong with Ruben Loftus-Cheek's added-time winner, Cardiff felt cheated.

They could have had the chance to make it 2-0 – and there was no way Azpilicueta's leveller should have stood – but assistant referee Eddie Smart kept his flag down.

The images of Warnock stood, hands on head, baffled at Pawson and his officiating team, would make the back pages the next day. "The best league in the worst and the worst referees," he told the television cameras afterwards, still seething.

The final whistle brought a chorus of boos around Cardiff City Stadium as Warnock – before his stare-off with Pawson – argued with Azpilicueta and Chelsea's David Luiz.

"Roll on VAR," was another Warnock quote from that day, referencing the video assisted refereeing technology that was being trialled around the world. The Premier League listened and introduced VAR for the 2019/20 season, but that was too late for Cardiff.

"So many things disappointed me in that league," Warnock says, looking back.

"The Chelsea thing killed us, we didn't deserve that. I'll never forget the dressing room after that game. I remember saying to Blacky and Ron [Kevin Blackwell and Ronnie Jepson], 'That's us done now'.

"I doubted whether the players would be able to recover

from it because we were five points adrift and we would have been two points adrift with some good games coming up. And we deserved to beat Chelsea, I didn't think they were ever in it."

As Warnock predicted, Cardiff didn't recover. They lost 2-0 at Burnley in another defining match in their relegation battle, another occasion on which they felt aggrieved by the referee. Mike Dean had given Cardiff a penalty for a Ben Mee handball but then overturned his own decision, before denying another possible spot-kick for the Bluebirds when Aron Gunnarsson appeared to have been fouled.

It was almost too much to bear for Warnock, with his history of grievances with the Premier League, and the Cardiff fans too, who at Turf Moor chanted their disapproval at the standard of officiating. Warnock had been fined £20,000 for his comments after the Chelsea game for "insinuating bias", as he now puts it.

And after the Burnley game? The officials admitted they had made a mistake this time.

Warnock now reveals: "We got a letter from the league saying, 'Yes, we agree with us, he should be offside' – but what good is that a week later? It's bloody scandalous."

During this time there was some heated debate about

whether Cardiff had simply been the recipients of more bad luck, or whether there was some sort of wider conspiracy against them.

Aled Blake believes officials in the Premier League often subconsciously favoured the bigger clubs, leaving the likes of Cardiff on the thin end of the wedge. "I genuinely feel like there was some kind of institutional bias against not just Cardiff City but smaller clubs in the Premier League," he says.

"We didn't get marginal decisions – that we might have got now with VAR – because refs are more likely to sway the way of an established and bigger club.

"Chelsea was the famous game of our season for all the wrong reasons. People still talk about it as the game that sealed our relegation fate – but which shouldn't have, we should have got something from it.

"It knocked the wind out of our sails, which hadn't been blowing very hard anyway! Warnock's reaction after it was how we all felt."

Bamba puts it more bluntly: "With VAR I think we would have stayed up."

Whatever fans thought about the refereeing decisions, not even another away victory could rescue Cardiff's season from here. They had won 2-0 at Brighton, thanks to Morrison and Nathaniel Mendez-Laing goals, to keep the beacon alight. But three more successive defeats in April – against Fulham, Liverpool and Crystal Palace – sealed their relegation. Ultimately Cardiff lost too much momentum, and perhaps confidence, as a result of the Chelsea and Burnley controversies.

* * * *

After the thrilling ride that had been the Championship promotion season and the excitement building up to the Premier League, the season hadn't fulfilled the desires of fans, players, nor Warnock himself. The veteran manager desperately wanted it to be different this time, but so much had stacked up against his troops. They couldn't prove the miracle.

For everyone connected with the club, however, there was a sense of pride at the end of all this. Cardiff City had done themselves justice throughout the most unimaginably difficult season – and more importantly they had done Emiliano Sala proud.

As Warnock said after relegation was confirmed with the 3-2 defeat to Palace: "They have kept fighting for me, so I have no complaints. It is what it is. I have nothing but praise for everyone, the fans have got behind us."

The loyal supporters enjoyed one more famous afternoon in the sunshine on the final day of the season when their side, playing with the handbrake off after relegation was already confirmed, went to Old Trafford and beat Manchester United 2-0.

To secure such a win, through a Mendez-Laing brace, was an enormously satisfying moment considering they had been denied points against the 'big six' earlier in the campaign. Plus there was the schadenfreude of inflicting a painful defeat on beleaguered United boss and familiar foe Ole Gunnar Solskjaer, in Man United's backyard.

Warnock was then joined by Ken Choo and all his players on the Manchester turf afterwards to applaud their supporters, who had cheered them on every step of the way. It remains the lasting Premier League memory for many fans.

But what was lingering in the back of many people's minds was the uncertainty and the pain of not knowing when Cardiff would be back. They had fought so hard to get there and to stay there, so the feeling was bittersweet.

"The disappointment, unfortunately, will always stop with me," Warnock still admits now. "I didn't think we deserved to go down. But early on in the season Chris Sutton and people like that – they were saying we weren't even going to get 11 points, we were going to be the worst team ever in the Premier League.

"So to see Fulham and Huddersfield down there, Fulham spending £120million and our wage bill was the lowest by a mile – 50 per cent of anybody else – and to get so close that will always stay with me as disappointment."

In the end, Cardiff had been relegated by just two points. They say an inch is as bad as a mile. But for a team who had gone to hell and back during an unprecedented season, it really wasn't bad going.

CHAPTER SEVENTEEN

What Happens Next?

The day after Cardiff City's 2-0 victory at Manchester United and the denouement of the Premier League season, Neil Warnock went to London to meet Mehmet Dalman and Ken Choo. There was lots on the agenda: Warnock's own future, the summer ahead and how Cardiff would plan for life back in the Championship.

Warnock retained the backing of supporters for the way he'd hauled them, thanks to his strong will and force of personality, through the Premier League campaign, albeit without the golden prize of staying in the division. He had been clapped and cheered off the pitch after the 3-2 defeat at home to Crystal Palace when Cardiff's relegation had been confirmed, and serenaded again at Old Trafford.

There was no doubt he had united a club regardless of the relegation, but the next task was rather more complex. It was the start of a new cycle.

The first problem was one that Warnock could have foreseen, as loan stars Victor Camarasa and Harry Arter returned to their parent clubs, while Aron Gunnarsson and Bruno Manga both left after Cardiff were unable to negotiate contract extensions.

The financial implications of relegation would be borne out in the longer term, but these were big losses in terms of the playing squad and Warnock had accepted in his press conference at Old Trafford there was serious work to be done in the 2019 summer transfer window.

The elephant in the room, however, was Warnock's own position, which was only briefly discussed during that London meeting.

In February 2018 he had signed a new contract to keep him at Cardiff until the end of the 2019/20 season, but relegation and the summer break presented the Bluebirds board with an opportunity to bring new energy to the manager's role.

It was an opportunity they turned down, opting to back Warnock's unrivalled Championship know-how for one more season. And the man himself had no intention of leaving either. Having brought the club together, he sensed the chance to restore Premier League status straight away.

WalesOnline's Cardiff City correspondent Glen Williams believes the lure of that ninth promotion and a desire to pay back his adoring Cardiff fans was behind Warnock's decision to stay.

"There was probably a natural conclusion point there, where he could have gone," he says of that summer.

"But they got so close to staying in the Premier League, I think maybe he felt he had a duty to steer them through what he knows from experience is a turbulent time, being relegated from the Premier League. He's experienced that more than once.

"So overseeing that was definitely part of it and with the Sala situation it'd been such a difficult year, I think he didn't want more upheaval for the club. And he loves the club, he rightly thought he was the steady pair of hands Cardiff needed to negotiate the coming down and target immediate promotion back to the Premier League."

The Championship is, of course, where Warnock tends to thrive. The contrast to his relationship with the Premier League couldn't be more stark, so it was another no-brainer. It felt like the start of his Cardiff challenge all over again – back in his kind of league. He was looking forward to rekindling his fiery relationship with fans of clubs like Bristol City and Nottingham Forest. But he could again do it with a smile, after the hardships of the 2018/19 campaign had taken away some of his love for the game.

"I've never been a fashionable manager and it's always easier to knock me or criticise my style," reflects Warnock.

"I'm never gonna be everybody's cup of tea. They say Marmite and that, but even the fans who don't like me, I think they respect me. We have a laugh and I always give stick back to them when they give it to me. And it's always been in good humour, which I think is missing from football.

"I think everybody is too serious now. I've never wanted that, I've always wanted to make sure I enjoy it and the fans enjoy it."

So Warnock saw the 2019/20 season as another chance to enjoy being manager of Cardiff City again, after a punishing season in the Premier League.

The problem was that the Championship doesn't allow passengers and it would be an almighty task to restore the Bluebirds' energy levels, while adding sufficient quality to mount another promotion bid.

After taking his squad on tour to the USA – a strange choice in many people's eyes, after touring Cornwall in the two previous summers – Warnock set about moulding another squad for promotion. He had to make major repairs to his defence, midfield and attack, after Kenneth Zohore, Kadeem Harris and Loic Damour joined Gunnarsson, Manga, Arter and Camarasa in departing.

Relegation from the Premier League often means major changes to a club's playing staff, but the number of departures threatened the balance of Warnock's squad. Incomings would be vital but Cardiff would struggle to maintain the level of quality they'd had.

Cardiff's first three confirmed signings of the summer were, perhaps inevitably, all rather understated. Welsh midfielder Will Vaulks signed from Warnock's old club Rotherham, while goalkeeper Joe Day and centre-back Curtis Nelson arrived from League Two and League One clubs, Newport and Oxford United respectively. All were promising players, but there was no doubt Cardiff were shopping in the lower leagues again.

Later in the window came the more high-profile signings, with Warnock securing centre-back Aden Flint and landing a big-money striker when paying £5.5million for German target man Robert Glatzel. It proved to be another busy summer with the further additions of Gavin Whyte – also from Oxford – and a double deadline day swoop for Birmingham forward Isaac Vassell and another Bristol City player, Marlon Pack.

Despite the number of signings, there were questions about the quality Cardiff had brought in and whether this was a promotion-winning squad being assembled.

"I don't think it was a particularly excellent transfer window," adds Williams. "There were a number of signings that on the surface seemed a bit strange.

"The signing of Joe Day still perplexes me. Marlon Park was an interesting one. I've spoken to Will Vaulks since and I think he was under the impression that Marlon Pack wasn't going to come in. [Vaulks] spent the first few months of the season, under Warnock, playing for the Under-23s and I think he was signed on the proviso that he was going to be a first-choice central midfielder. Then they suddenly signed Pack on deadline day.

"With Isaac Vassell, I think Warnock signed him on a bit of a whim. He was someone [Warnock] liked when he played for Truro City... I know you get gut feelings about players, but everyone raised an eyebrow at that one.

"They signed Glatzel who was a bit of an unknown quantity and people were crying out for some reassurance that they were going to sign an experienced Championship striker, so if Glatzel didn't work they could fall back on someone else. Vassell has only scored a handful of Championship goals in his career."

What baffled many supporters most was the decision to let Bobby Decordova-Reid join Fulham in the final hours of deadline day, on loan, with a view to a £10million deal, which was later made permanent. Decordova-Reid, like Josh Murphy, had been signed the summer before as a long-term option, someone who would thrive in the Championship if Cardiff went down.

But after an up and down 2018/19 campaign when he'd often found himself on the bench, Decordova-Reid opted to join Arter at Craven Cottage, who had been relegated alongside the Bluebirds.

Cardiff supporters felt deflated. Their side had lost some seriously talented players and they didn't feel reassured that the new boys would be good enough.

"Before Decordova-Reid's exit I think it was in the balance," says Williams. "It wasn't too bad a window, although it wasn't excellent, but there was still firepower. When he went, I got the sense of an immediate shift from the fanbase.

"Until then the message from board level was, 'We're

going to have a stronger squad than what was promoted last time', but after the departure of Decordova-Reid a lot of people then thought that wasn't the case."

Warnock was happy enough, feeling he could again work his magic with a squad that was prepared to be disciplined and humble, as before. The old spine was still there too: Sean Morrison, Neil Etheridge, Joe Ralls, Sol Bamba – although the latter was still injured. Junior Hoilett and Nathaniel Mendez-Laing were ready to fire again and there were high hopes that Glatzel could finally be the answer up front.

But the start of a season is so important if you're gunning for promotion, as Cardiff proved in 2017/18. Results in August and September this time around were a mixed bag. There was no momentum.

Williams argues the 3-0 defeat to Reading on 18th August, the third game of the season, was an early warning sign, as Cardiff capitulated, stopped fighting. The spirit just didn't seem the same as before.

Had things gone stale under Warnock?

After the drubbing at the Madejski Stadium, the Cardiff manager thought briefly after quitting there and then, having to be talked round by his captain Morrison after the game. But Warnock remained despondent: he had just watched a performance that no longer resembled one of his teams. Finding the unifying spirit of 2017/18 was proving much more difficult after relegation and a summer of change.

* * * *

Their results showed few signs of turning, despite the reintroduction of Lee Tomlin to the playmaking role – in the absence of Camarasa and Decordova-Reid – with some success. For every 3-0 win over QPR, there was a 4-2 defeat at West Brom. There were too many draws as well for a team targeting promotion, six in the opening 14 games of the season. Cardiff's defence was wildly inconsistent without Bamba and Manga.

"Manga was especially missed," adds Williams, as £4million signing Flint struggled.

"At first I thought Flint was brilliant. But when things go wrong he's the sort of player who made mistakes look far worse, he stands out because he's big and cumbersome. It was a poor signing and people were comparing him to Bruno Manga, who was twice the player."

Glatzel also floundered, scoring just two goals in his

first 11 appearances, with Tomlin – bizarrely – the only bright spark for Cardiff. Tomlin and Warnock's relationship had been through the ringer, the playmaker was dismissed as unsuitable for the manager's style of play, then sent out on loan to Nottingham Forest and Peterborough United. But Tomlin had worked hard on his fitness in the summer of 2019 and vowed to turn his Cardiff fortunes around.

But his journey from outcast to key player in a matter of weeks at the start of the season was, for many, a sign that this was no longer a Warnock team in its truest form.

"It was less by design and more by necessity," Williams explains. "Having to choose Tomlin speaks more about how the team wasn't equipped as it should have been.

"Because if Warnock had his way I don't think he would have picked Tomlin. He tried to sell him in the summer."

But not even a revitalised Tomlin could paper over the cracks. Cardiff's squad had serious weaknesses that were being regularly exposed. And as such, Warnock's own doubts, which had crept in that night at Reading, would resurface after further poor results in September and October.

One of Warnck's regular habits was to read everything

about his club, even delving into the fan forums and newspaper columns – through the good periods and the bad. But when times are tough the comments become a little more difficult to swallow. The criticism was beginning to outstrip the praise. It started to sting.

"That's probably been my downfall as well, because I listened to those when I left," Warnock now says.

"I probably read too much into it. And I always said if they started to question things, then let's leave them on a high because we don't want to leave them on a low. And good luck to them.

"It was just the bitterness from some of them on the forums, without naming names. And some of the accusations as well, they were quite derogatory. It just left a nasty taste in the mouth, really."

It didn't get any easier for Warnock, as derby defeats to Swansea City and then Bristol City left Cardiff's promotion chances remote to zero. In both games the Bluebirds lost tamely 1-0, without the spirit and fight of old.

In the early months of his Cardiff reign Warnock would joke about tearing up his contract if the fans started booing him. He didn't need that at his age, he would say. His carefree manner was refreshing, part of his charm.

WHAT HAPPENS NEXT?

But now it was a serious consideration. Having gone through so much with the Bluebirds, he didn't want to spoil his wonderful memories of the club and that special relationship he had with supporters.

"I thought at the end of the day I'd done my bit, now let somebody else come in," he adds. "Sometimes the grass isn't always greener. Now I'll do something else."

That's exactly what he did. It was time to go.

A win over Bristol City in his first game in charge, a defeat to Bristol City in his last game. There was even a wry smile between Warnock and old foe Lee Johnson as they shook hands after the defeat on 10th November. So he took his destiny in his own hands and it wasn't a shock when the announcement soon followed.

"By mutual consent" often means a sacking in football parlance, but it was accurate this time. Warnock's friend Mehmet Dalman understood his position and reluctantly agreed to let him go. It was as amicable as a managerial departure could be.

"I didn't want to get kicked out with booing or anything because I didn't want to remember it like that," says Warnock. "I know it was only a few of the fans and when I left I was inundated with letters and stuff saying how sorry they were that I went."

A tough summer transfer window, a feeling of after the lord mayor's show, a loss of the unity of previous years, the reasons for Warnock's eventual demise at Cardiff were nuanced. But they were also simple: he had reached the end of the road. Maybe he should have gone in the summer, but it was typical of Warnock to want another crack at promotion due to the lure of taking Cardiff back to the big time.

It wasn't to be. The Bluebirds appointed former Millwall manager Neil Harris as his replacement, a younger man with fresh ideas but also someone who would keep the ethos of Warnock's Cardiff at the heart of everything. With promotion now improbable and Cardiff in 14th position in the league, the club saw an opportunity to rebuild under Harris.

Yet some believed Warnock should have been kept on at the club in some capacity, in an advisory or director role, having unified the club.

"It's a kick in the teeth in the end," says Nathan Blake. "I don't think Neil deserved what happened. While being loyal to the club, what he did in recorrecting the position of the club and putting it back to pieces, he should have been offered something, offered the chance to work with a coach who put in place more progressive football.

WHAT HAPPENS NEXT?

"The club has since found getting to the Premier League is not as easy as Neil found it to be."

Cardiff's position did improve under Harris, who eventually secured a fifth-place finish, falling short in the play-offs. But the new boss initially found it tough, while Warnock enjoyed a spell of much-needed downtime at his Cornwall home. Despite being touted for an immediate return to management – with jobs at Hearts, Bolton, Ipswich among others – he was now 71 and needed time to reflect, though not for too long.

Middlesbrough came calling in June 2020 after sacking Jonathan Woodgate and Warnock couldn't resist a return to the Championship. The rescheduled league season, moved into the summer and played behind closed doors due to the global coronavirus pandemic, meant he was given eight games to rescue Boro from relegation.

A familiar challenge for him and Kevin Blackwell and Ronnie Jepson, who again joined his backroom staff. And it would prove a familiar outcome, with Warnock eventually leading Boro to a respectable 17th position, five points clear of the relegation zone.

Yet it was telling that he had almost a year away from management. Warnock was hurt, exhausted and elements of his Cardiff tenure still irked him: the Emiliano Sala tragedy, the Chelsea game, the agonising two-point gap to safety. But the overriding emotion was pride, even after it all unravelled.

"I do enjoy challenges, and the challenge is to get the team higher up the league and see where we go," Warnock had said in his first Cardiff City press conference in October 2016.

Not even a manager of his 40-year experience could have foreseen the challenges that were to come over the next three years. It had been an amazing journey.

Epilogue

How much does a managerial legacy matter?

If you're Neil Warnock and your task at Cardiff City was to overhaul a Championship club and take it into the Premier League – and you achieved that aim – then maybe it doesn't matter very much at all. You can reflect on a job well done.

Warnock's appointment had been a shrewd but short-term option taken up by the Cardiff board and it paid off in fine style, with almost immediate success on the pitch and a swell of good feeling off the field. The latter remained despite the anticlimactic way in which it all came to a conclusion.

And while in many ways Warnock's brand of effective football didn't leave a lasting legacy, as he invested energy into first-team results rather than academy development, his personality left a lasting imprint on the club.

It had been apparent from the start that this was a manager of the Cardiff people. Within months of his appointment, an enormous image of Warnock adorned the side of Cardiff City Stadium, while his words "my kind of club, my kind of people" became a club slogan.

As supporter Aled Blake admits: "In terms of the fanbase his legacy is enormous and will never be forgotten "

The players he brought in, Sol Bamba, Junior Hoilett, Nathaniel Mendez-Laing and Neil Etheridge in particular, plus the ones he shaped in Sean Morrison, Joe Ralls, Aron Gunnarsson and Bruno Manga, will always be remembered by fans as key members of that 2018 promotion-winning side. The sun-soaked, blue-clad promotion celebrations of that wonderful day will be forever etched in history. For those reasons, Warnock's place in the sun is assured.

But it was the way he spoke, his good humour in dealing with people and his connection with the fans that will stay with people more than anything specifically about the football. He often likened that little spot of South Wales to his Yorkshire roots and Cardiff became his spiritual home.

"Thousands of Cardiff City fans will always thank him for what he did," says Glen Williams. "In terms of a legacy I think the vast majority of fans remember he brought the club and the fans closer together again.

"And while some people might hold gripes over how Warnock neglected the academy and youth system, I think most recognise how much he did.

"I'm sure if he ever came back for a game and was paraded in front of the fans, he'd get a rip-roaring applause."

It's for this same reason why Warnock still has ties with the first professional club he ever managed, in 1980, Gainsborough Trinity; and why he regularly returns to Scarborough for charity dinners, why fans of QPR, Huddersfield, Notts County and Sheffield United still hold him in such high esteem.

When Warnock was unveiled as Middlesbrough manager, there was no ill-feeling from Cardiff fans, only goodwill towards him, despite the fact he had taken a job at a Championship rival.

Humility is an underrated quality in his management and stems from his own childhood as a Sheffield United fan, where his love for football grew thanks to his father.

Warnock tells one tale of being turned down by a

Blades player for an autograph as a boy and from that day forward vowed to always remember his fans when he became a player and manager himself.

"I'll never forget waiting at Bramall Lane for a player to sign an autograph. I was only in short trousers," he says.

"He came out and ran across and said, 'Sorry son, I'm in such a rush'. I was wet through, I'd been waiting two hours and I cried on my way home. So when I first started playing football my dad said, 'If anyone asks you for an autograph, make sure you sign it'.

"I always ask my players to sign a few autographs when they get off the bus. I hate it when the lads have the big earphones on and they go straight in and don't even bother. It's almost like people forget the fans and I'll never forget that disappointment I felt as a kid, so I'll always stop for 10 minutes and have a laugh with the fans around the bus because they're the bread and butter.

"It's when they stop asking you that it's time to worry, which is why I always made time for that."

His affable manner in dealing with journalists, too, ensures a fair and predominantly positive coverage, especially in the local press, which Warnock recognises is the mouthpiece of his supporters. In the modern era he's one of a small minority of managers who speaks directly to the media, rather than go through a press officer conduit.

Like his managerial idol Brian Clough, and his mentor Len Ashurst, who managed Warnock when he was a player at Hartlepool – and also had spells in charge of Cardiff – Warnock is unashamedly old-school. The Bluebirds fans, and the Cardiff-covering press pack, appreciated that in an era of mundane jargonistic managers.

"It's changed a lot nowadays and not for the better. But when I was brought up, we took our local journalist on the bus with us," Warnock says.

"And we told him everything. We'd say, 'You can print that, but don't print that'. He was almost one of your staff. But then pressure has come on journalists for headlines and tabloids have changed over the last 15 and 20 years and as a manager you can get stitched up if you're not careful. So you become wary and don't tell them as much.

"But I've always thought if someone's got a job to do, if I can I'll always ring them back."

From a personal point of view, I appreciated Warnock's courtesy in calling me back, often to tell me I was wrong about a player's match rating, or to inform me of the next day's team news. It's one of the reasons I've been able to write this book, thanks to his honesty and insight. For a young journalist making their way in the industry it was helpful and a great mark of the respect Warnock showed to everyone he came across.

Having worked closely with him, I feel Warnock's reputation in the wider public doesn't always paint an accurate picture of him as a manager, as Cardiff City fans will attest. He is warm, he is charismatic and he is humorous – you don't see that side to him when he's haranguing referees or opposition players, or complaining to the TV cameras after a defeat.

But he's also uber-competitive, an expert at eking out results, a manager who at almost every club he's taken charge of, has taken them on an upward trajectory.

His Cardiff reign is notable because it may prove to be his last hurrah at the top level. But it's also exemplary of his ability to drive a club forward through inspiration and motivation.

It's Warnock's knack of getting the best out of his players that stands out more than anything else, but he does this through his amiable personality. It's why players like Paddy Kenny, Shaun Derry, Clint Hill, Junior Hoilett and Brian Murphy have been compelled to work with him at multiple clubs. It's why Greg Halford thanks

him for giving him the best season of his career, why Sol
Bamba consults Warnock on all his major life decisions.

Warnock builds bonds with players and that forms
the nucleus of a club's togetherness. There was no better
example of this than his relationship with Bamba at
Cardiff City.

"He knows my wife, knows my kids and I feel I can talk
to him about anything," says Bamba. "Every time I've
had a big decision to make with regards to family, money
or anything, I go to him first. He's been as good as gold
and it goes way beyond football."

Perhaps that is the greatest endorsement of Neil
Warnock's time as manager of Cardiff City. To him, it
wasn't just about the game of football, it was about being
a good person and that helped him bring a city together,
unite a fanbase previously at war with itself and inspire a
playing staff that was low on energy and desire.

"I always used to call it 'muck and nettles' and that's
how it felt," he says. "It was ironic, Bristol City my first
game and Bristol City my last and the journey in between
has just been amazing. I think 99.9 per cent of fans have
enjoyed the ride. They've all been to the fairground,
they've got on the helter skelter and they've got memories
– more good ones than bad ones. And that's my legacy."

For ardent Bluebirds fans, watching their team has always been a way of life, more than just a game. To them, football is escapism, their weekend enjoyment, and Warnock identified with that. His main objective, then, was to send the crowd home with something to talk about every week.

And for more than three years, there was no shortage of entertainment at Cardiff City. It was always his kind of club.